Careers in Management Consulting

2007 Edition

WetFeet Insider Guide

WetFeet®

Helping you make smarter career decisions.

WetFeet, Inc.

The Folger Building
101 Howard Street
Suite 300
San Francisco, CA 94105

Phone: (415) 284-7900 or 1-800-926-4JOB
Fax: (415) 284-7910
Website: www.wetfeet.com

Careers in Management Consulting

2007 Edition
ISBN: 1-58207-644-2

Table of Contents

Management Consulting at a Glance

Opportunity Overview

- Undergrads from all majors are heavily recruited for two- to three-year positions as analysts.

- MBAs compete for a large number of tenure-track slots at all firms.

- Many firms court JDs, PhDs, and other advanced-degree holders.

- Midcareer people are hired on an ad hoc basis into various levels by most firms.

Major Advantages of Careers in Consulting

- Excellent opportunity to learn about a wide variety of businesses and business issues

- Work with a talented, fun, and hardworking group of people

- Outstanding pay and perks

Major Disadvantages of Careers in Consulting

- Long, intense work hours (55 to 60 per week on average) and lots of travel

- Your life's not your own—it belongs to your clients

- A step or two removed from actual decision-making and profit/loss responsibility. Consultants can only make suggestions; they can't guarantee that those suggestions will be successfully implemented.

Recruiting Overview

- Formalized and competitive process

- Primary channel is on-campus recruiting

- Emphasis on academic and analytical abilities

- Case interviews mandatory for most firms (and painful if you're not prepared)

What Recruiters Look For

- On resumes, recruiters typically look for evidence of communication skills, quantitative aptitude, leadership ability, and academic achievement.

- In interviews, recruiters want to know how students think; they encourage candidates to be themselves, to answer questions directly and honestly, and to explain their thinking clearly.

- Recruiters agree that students who succeed in consulting have strong problem-solving skills, work well in teams, and share a commitment to helping clients.

The Industry

Overview

So, you're about to graduate and you think you want to be a management consultant. Or, more likely, you think you'll spend a few years as a consultant and then move on to other things. You're not alone. Consulting firms are traditionally among the largest employers of top MBAs and college graduates, and competition for jobs is stiff every year.

More than half the people in top MBA programs and a significant number of college seniors flirt with the idea of becoming a management consultant after graduation. It's a high-paying, high-profile field that offers students the opportunity to take on a lot of responsibility right out of school and quickly learn a great deal about the business world.

In essence, consultants are hired advisors to corporations. They tackle a wide variety of business problems and provide solutions for their clients. Depending on the size and chosen strategy of the firm, these problems can be as straightforward as researching a new market or as complex as totally rethinking the client's organization. No matter what the project is, the power that management consultants wield is hard to scoff at. They can advise a client to acquire a company worth hundreds of millions of dollars, or to reduce the size of its workforce by thousands of employees.

The big names in management consulting are well known. Bain & Company, the Boston Consulting Group, McKinsey & Company, and a solid crop of similar firms vie for contracts from the Fortune 500. Each firm has a slightly different focus, culture, and approach. Pay attention to these differences so you can show in your interviews that you understand why Company X is far superior to the rest of the field, and what makes you the perfect fit. We provide a few pointers in this book to help you distinguish between the players. Insiders throughout the industry stress that knowing the differences between firm practices and cultures is critical to getting hired. For those of you interested in a closer look at a particular firm, WetFeet publishes the company Insider Guide series. See www.wetfeet.com for a full list of guides.

One word of clarification: "Consulting" is a big, one-size-fits-all term that includes virtually any form of advice-giving in a business setting. This book focuses primarily on the flavor known as management consulting. Often called strategy consulting, this segment of the industry includes firms that specialize in providing advice about strategic and core operational issues, such as finding new channels for selling products or reducing the costs involved in producing a product. Although some of the highest-profile firms populate this segment, they're not the only ones doing consulting.

Thousands of other organizations and individuals call themselves consultants, make money by selling their advisory services, and offer plenty of opportunities for employment. If you like the idea of advising businesses, and you have a particular interest in computers, human resources, corporate communications, mobile communications, health care, financial services, real estate, e-commerce, or some other specialized field, there's a good chance that you can find a position with an organization doing precisely that.

IT services, in particular, has grown up over the past decade. Many of the biggest consulting firms, including IBM Global Services, Capgemini, and Accenture, derive a significant portion of their revenue through systems integration and outsourcing engagements. These firms work with a client to develop hardware and software solutions and then often manage the systems (hence the term outsourcing).

By and large, the things insiders like about consulting are similar across the board. They enjoy the variety afforded by working in different industries for many different clients, the intellectual challenge of pushing themselves to the limit as they tackle complex business problems, and the people with whom they work. And they like the money and the perks. The industry pays very well, and consultants travel in style.

Consulting insiders also offer a litany of complaints: 60-hour workweeks are standard (with crunch times often calling for more), extended travel is the rule, and personal plans must often be put on hold. "The deadlines are driven by the clients and not by you," says an insider. That's not a complaint; it's a fact—be aware of it. In addition, at some point most consultants long for the opportunity to actually implement their great ideas.

The Bottom Line

Consulting is a fantastic long-term career for a few, a great short-term experience for many more, and the wrong place for many others. The work is challenging and diverse, but it's a step removed from actually operating a company. It requires intellect, people skills, and a willingness to work hard. The pay is outstanding, especially if you're in one of the well-known firms. While just about anybody with a few good skills can find work as a consultant of one sort or another, competition for jobs at the elite firms is particularly intense. "Really do your research. Do you think this is going to be the right environment, the right career? Consulting can be invigorating, but it's very challenging as well," says one insider. Says another, "Don't do this job for the money. Do it because you have an insatiable intellectual curiosity, a passion for solving problems, and you like variety."

Know why you want to be a consultant, know why you want to work at the firms you're applying to, and make sure every piece of correspondence you send to a firm is customized in this way—oh, and your spelling and grammar had better be perfect, too.

Outlook

Overall, the management consulting industry outlook is positive. Around 44 percent of firms saw double-digit growth in 2005; mid-way through 2006, about half the firms anticipate double-digit growth in 2006, according to *Consultants News*. "Based on what I'm seeing in this business, things are really happening," says an insider. Another notes there is deal flow across the board: "The economy overall seems to be doing really well."

Insiders report heavy recruiting in 2006 for the second year in a row. The Boston Consulting Group reportedly brought in its largest class ever. Booz Allen reported that competition for recruits was similar to the situation in the late 1990s. This competition for graduates reflects several trends, including a shrinking number of students earning MBAs; more competition from other industries, such as technology firms, financial services, real estate, and government agencies; and voluntary attrition typical of a strong economy, as consultants leave for new opportunities. These trends bode well for the class of 2006–07.

This doesn't mean that getting a job will be easy. "I would guesstimate that on average, less than 90 percent of the people who interview with consulting firms get an offer," says an insider. "You have to be ready to play the game and really prepare for the interview process." The insider advises applicants to "interview with as many firms as you can. There are a lot of good firms." Don't get caught in the misperception that if you don't go to a top firm, you shouldn't go into consulting. You might be surprised by a smaller firm you didn't think about at first. And be sure you know why you want to work in the industry. "Don't do this job for the money," cautions an insider. "Do it because you have an insatiable intellectual curiosity, a passion for solving problems, and you like variety."

Be aware of the changing dynamics of the industry as well. It's become more mature; the major sectors—IT, HR, strategy, and operations—are increasingly becoming a specialty market with growth drivers unconnected to the other sectors. Meanwhile, clients have grown savvier, in some cases creating their own in-house consulting teams, which has put pressure on billing rates and increased demand for consultants with industry experience. "For the pre-MBA experience, it would be advantageous to make sure [candidates are] getting some serious, substantial experience—industry experience for the type of client engagements they want to work in post-MBA," an insider says. "Some MBAs will look at the summer associate program as an opportunity to try something completely different. But if they're trying something for variety, and they want to work in a post-MBA position in a field different than their summer position, they're putting themselves at a disadvantage."

Industry Rankings

The consulting industry doesn't lend itself to easy numerical comparisons. First, many firms are privately held, so revenue and profit figures aren't readily available. Second, there's considerable disagreement over what constitutes consulting revenue. Do we consider all of the fee income or only management consulting revenue? How do we handle firms that have several different business units that provide consulting? Third, firms operate in a wide variety of sectors, from outsourcing IT to strategy, which makes it challenging to classify industry players. For instance, it's clear that McKinsey is a management consulting firm, but what about IBM, which has a large systems consulting group? All this is to say that you should pick your own favorite number, decide what it means to you, and be sure to take it with a grain of salt.

The rankings following are from an annual Universum and *Fortune* survey of MBAs who named the companies they'd most like to work for in 2006, and *Consulting Magazine*'s annual survey of top consulting employers (which are not ranked).

On *Fortune*'s list, McKinsey landed in first place for the tenth year in a row; Bain and BCG held steady. With the exception of Monitor and Mercer, all of the rest of the firms saw their ranking fall in this year's survey. But it wasn't all bad news for the industry: after seeing the percentage of candidates who said they'd like to work in the consulting industry fall from 25 percent in 2004 to 23 percent in 2005, the number was back up to 25 percent in 2006 (holding steady at 22 percent for women, and climbing three percentage points to 28 percent for men). This was the highest percentage of all the sectors.

WHERE MBAS WANT TO WORK, 2006

Consulting Firms that Ranked in the Fortune Top 100 MBA Employers

Rank	Firm
1	McKinsey & Company
4	Bain & Company
5	The Boston Consulting Group
15	Booz Allen Hamilton
17	Deloitte (includes consulting and audit units)
23	IBM Corporation (includes whole company, not just Global Services)
43	Accenture Ltd
50	PricewaterhouseCoopers
63	A.T. Kearney
68	Monitor Company Group
78	Mercer
100	BearingPoint

Source: Based on a study by Universum; http://money.cnn.com/magazines/fortune/mba100/.

Consulting Magazine's Ten Best Consulting Firms to Work For, 2005

Firm
Bain & Company
Booz Allen Hamilton
The Boston Consulting Group
DiamondCluster International
Kurt Salmon Associates
McKinsey & Company
Mercer Management Consulting
Mercer Oliver Wyman
Pittiglio Rabin Todd & McGrath
Sapient

Source: *Consulting Magazine.*

Firm Thumbnails, 2005

Firm	World Mgmt. Consulting Revenue ($M)	Professionals (World)	# of Projects at Once	Favored Location for Work
Accenture	15,550	129,000	1	Client
Advisory Board Company	159	750	Varies	Office
A.T. Kearney	n/a	3,000	1	Client
Bain & Company	n/a	2,400	2	Office
BearingPoint	n/a	16,800	2	Client
Booz Allen Hamilton (WCB)	3,500	17,000	1	Client
The Boston Consulting Group	1,500	2,900	2	Office
Capgemini	9,847	60,000	1	Client
CGI Group	3,685	25,000	1	Varies
Computer Sciences Corporation	14,610	80,000	1	Client
Corporate Executive Board Corporation	362	1,865	Varies	Varies
Deloitte Consulting	4,300	n/a	1	Client
DiamondCluster International	193	751	1	Client
IBM Global Services	47,400	190,000	Varies	Varies
L.E.K.	n/a	500	2	Varies
Marakon Associates	n/a	300	n/a	Client
McKinsey & Company	n/a	n/a	1	Client
Mercer Management Consulting	909	1,000	1	Client
Monitor Company Group	n/a	n/a	2	Office
Navigant Consulting	576	1,700	1	n/a
PRTM	n/a	500	1–2	Varies
Roland Berger Strategy Consultants GmbH	n/a	,630	1	Client

Notes: All numbers are estimates based on information from publicly available sources. Different firms count professional employees differently. Fiscal years differ among firms; revenue and professionals are current as of spring 2005. Privately held firms do not disclose revenues.
Source: WetFeet research

The Big Picture

Sometimes it may seem like just about everybody professes to be a consultant. "Hold on," you say. "How can Aunt Suzie, who has her own consulting business, and those people in the blue suits at the famous New York addresses all be doing the same thing?" All of them might really be consultants, but you can bet they're not all doing the same thing. Just as there are many different sorts of doctors, there are consultants with all manner of expertise and specialty.

As mentioned, this report deals primarily with management consultancies, the elite consulting firms that make the most money advising the biggest and most powerful companies in the world. However, there are a number of specialized groups within the management consulting field and many more types of consulting firms that provide specialized advice and services in other areas.

People who want a career in consulting can find a number of attractive choices. To help you get a better handle on the options, we've grouped the consulting world into several segments. Keep in mind, however, that our groupings are flexible. Firms in one group can and do compete directly with players in other segments. Also, consolidation, growth, and market gyrations rapidly change the landscape. One final caveat: Where we've placed a firm does not reflect the quality of the organization. Brief profiles of a few of the major categories follow.

ELITE MANAGEMENT CONSULTING FIRMS

This group is populated by a few top strategy firms—Bain, Booz Allen, BCG, McKinsey—and a host of smaller challengers. The bulk of the work done by these firms consists of providing strategic or operational advice to top executive officers in Fortune 500 companies. For this, they charge the highest fees and enjoy the most prestige. They also have the biggest attitudes, work the most intense hours, and take home the most pay. The elite management consulting firms fight to woo the top graduates from the best graduate and undergraduate schools. Although some elite firms differentiate themselves by specializing in particular industries or functions, most consultants who work for these firms are generalists who work on a wide variety of projects and industries.

Representative firms: Accenture, A.T. Kearney, Bain & Company, Booz Allen Hamilton, The Boston Consulting Group, Marakon Associates, Mercer Management Consulting, McKinsey & Company, Monitor Group

BIG FOUR–AFFILIATED CONSULTING FIRMS

The Big Four were the Big Five until Andersen went bankrupt after the Enron scandal in 2002, driving what at the time seemed to be the final stake into the heart of a historically lucrative marriage between consultants and auditors. When Andersen went bankrupt, consulting firms were already separating from their audit partners: Ernst & Young had sold its consulting practice to Cap Gemini to form Cap Gemini Ernst & Young (now Capgemini), and KPMG Consulting had broken off from its accounting side and gone public (now known as BearingPoint). Other members of this group include PricewaterhouseCoopers, which sold its consulting unit to IBM in July 2002, and Deloitte Consulting, where a buyout by consulting partners was scotched (the consulting arm has since been reintegrated into Deloitte). These firms have started rebuilding their consulting practices, and they're worth keeping an eye on—noncompete agreements (which prohibit the audit firms from crossing business lines into consulting services) for KPMG and PricewaterhouseCoopers run out in 2006 and 2007, respectively, and E&Y's is already up, which means these firms can get back into the consulting game, and could be hiring. (Deloitte never did divest its consulting arm.) The Big Four firms offer strategic business and operations advice and other more specialized consulting services, such as advice about regulatory requirements, to many of the same corporations served by the elite consulting firms.

BOUTIQUE STRATEGY FIRMS

Within the universe of business strategy and operations, boutique consulting firms constitute a significant subgroup of firms that specialize in a particular industry, process, or type of consulting, such as litigation support, high-tech operations, or the pharmaceutical industry. Although it encompasses too many firms to name, this group includes players that have expertise in numerous fields. If you're interested in a specific industry or type of consulting, these firms offer excellent career opportunities. Typically, they're smaller than the big-name strategy firms and work with a more narrowly focused group of clients—so they won't usually require you to work in industries that don't interest you. Insiders tell us that working for one of these firms may give you more marketable experience if you decide to leave the world of consulting.

Representative firms: Cornerstone Research (litigation support), Gartner (high-tech research), Pittiglio Rabin Todd & McGrath (high-tech operations), Putnam Associates (pharmaceuticals, biotechnology, and medical devices)

TECHNOLOGY AND SYSTEMS CONSULTING FIRMS

If you're technologically inclined and love designing computer systems and applications, this might be the area for you. Firms here typically take on large projects to design, implement, and manage their clients' information and computer systems. In contrast to pie-in-the-sky strategy consulting, which involves work that can often be done at the home office, technology consulting often takes place in the bowels of the client organization. A typical project might involve creating a new inventory tracking system for a national retailer. Such a project might include analyzing the client's informational needs, acquiring new hardware, writing computer code to run the new system, and syncing the systems to deliver information in real time over the Internet. In general, this kind of consulting job requires large teams of people who actually do the computer work. As a result, there are usually more opportunities for people from undergraduate or technical backgrounds than from MBA backgrounds, but it's not the same high-prestige work strategy consultants are known for. Technology and systems firms have also moved aggressively to take on business-process outsourcing in order to manage elements of a client's business, such as a call center. In most cases, these jobs pay less than those at the top strategy firms.

Firms in this sector continue to hire in the United States, despite many jobs moving overseas—though some experts are concerned that outsourcing will drain more jobs from the U.S. There has been good news, though; one *InformationWeek* analysis showed that from 2004 to 2005, the United States gained 128,000 jobs in IT.

Representative firms: Accenture, BearingPoint, Capgemini, Computer Sciences Corporation (CSC), Electronic Data Systems Corporation (EDS), HP Technology Solutions Group, IBM Global Services, Novell, Oracle, SAP, Synopsis, Unisys

HUMAN RESOURCES CONSULTING

Technology's not your thing? How about the other end of the spectrum? A number of firms specialize in providing human resources consulting. This can include everything from designing an employee evaluation and compensation system to conducting organizational effectiveness training to helping a firm through a significant change event, such as a merger. Because such work is so important, HR consulting firms often work with relatively senior employees at client organizations. The firms hire MBAs and undergrads, but they also have an interest in people from other master's programs, especially those with training in HR management and organizational design and effectiveness. HR consultants often work as long and travel as much as their counterparts in general management consulting.

Representative firms: Accenture (Change Management Group), Buck Consultants, Deloitte, Hay Group, Hewitt Associates, Mercer Human Resource Consulting, Towers Perrin, Watson Wyatt Worldwide

Trends in Consulting

Each consulting firm has its own set of new programs and developments. However, you should familiarize yourself with a number of industry-wide trends. If you're interested in a particular firm, explore the role the following industry trends are playing in its practice.

A NEW, AND DIFFERENT, WAR FOR TALENT

The War for Talent first made news during the dotcom boom, as double-digit growth created strong demand for consulting services while lucrative (though often speculative) dotcom opportunities lured graduates away from consulting careers. During that period, voluntary turnover rates at many consulting firms were in the 20- to 25-percent range. After the dotcom crash and resulting economic downturn, voluntary turnover fell to the single-digits. With the resurgence in the economy—and new opportunities across industry sectors—consultants are leaving in higher-than-average numbers. And while the number of consultants leaving firms is down slightly in 2006 over 2005, voluntary attrition remains high, as a strong economy creates attractive opportunities for consultants outside of the large management consulting firms.

Meanwhile, firms are working hard to grow revenues—and with billing rates generally stagnant and only beginning to rise, they need people to do it. As a result, competition among firms for top candidates has been stiff. About half the firms expect to grow revenues by double-digit numbers in 2006— a promising shift that should give job seekers plenty to get excited about. And it's a welcome sight for graduates, who not only can expect more job opportunities, but better pay, as signing bonuses and base salaries are moving up.

EXPANDING ALTERNATIVES

Consulting firms are facing a new array of recruitment challenges on campuses. In this year's *Fortune* ranking of top employers for MBAs, Google—which wasn't on the list last year—slid into the number-two spot. Other technology companies, including Apple Computer, Microsoft, Intel, and Yahoo, all saw their rankings improve. Government agencies and real estate and law firms have beefed up recruiting on campus as well. "One thing for sure, clients are increasingly more capable—they tap into business school and hire people with MBAs," says an insider. "Things that used to be cutting edge with consulting aren't anymore. You have to innovate ahead of what your client is able to do, otherwise you're just an extra pair of hands, which you can get money for, but not a whole lot."

Many corporations have created leadership development programs to attract talented graduates, offering compelling, high-profile work, without all the travel and with better hours than consulting firms. These opportunities, and those in other industries, are worth looking at, and may be attractive if you're about to graduate. However, consulting still remains a unique industry for the range of opportunities and experiences it provides. "One thing that consulting offers, nobody will say to you in a future job interview, 'why did you go work at BCG?' It gives you a lot more flexibility than these other programs can really offer."

GROWTH SECTORS

In 2006, high growth areas include energy, utilities, and chemicals; health care; financial services; and public sector. (Says an insider newbie at an elite strategy firm: My firm "is not going to be a public sector firm, but I've heard more about it than I thought I was going to hear.") A number of insiders report an increase in enterprise resource planning (ERP) engagements, on both the IT and strategy sides. ERP systems integrate and automate business practices, such as payroll or ordering. Look for moderate growth in consumer packaged goods, communications and media, business services, and pharmaceuticals.

Asia continues to come on strong. Analysts reckon that companies in China need to apprentice some 75,000 executives who can work in a global market over the next five years if they want to meet growth targets; they have only 3,000 to 5,000 today. "Dealing with growth and change opportunities in China is on our mind," says a consultant. Firms have been bolstering their Asian practices to meet demand there; McKinsey, for instance, saw hiring in Asia increase from 15 percent last year to 20 percent in 2006.

EXTERNALITIES AND CSR

A few of the insiders we spoke to in 2006 mentioned the growing role of externalities in consulting engagements—consideration of things outside the engagement that could affect the industry sector, such as rising energy prices brought on by declining rates of oil production, the economic consequences of global warming, or the long-term health effects of a specific chemical or product. Understanding and planning and accounting for externalities has been a growing concern among many global businesses, as they can often affect cost of goods (the way rising oil prices affect the price of plastics and distribution), government regulation (which can force client businesses to change practices), and the bottom line (such as with lawsuits for a faulty or harmful product).

Similarly, corporate social responsibility (CSR) regularly ranks as a top concern for CEOs, and is an issue consulting firms can often play a role in addressing. "It's definitely a hot issue," says an insider. CSR issues range widely, from executive pay policies and treatment of workers overseas or the amount of CO_2 gases the company produces to philanthropic activities.

TECH FIRMS JOIN THE CONSULTANTS

Computer hardware and software firms continue to elbow their way into consulting through business process outsourcing—wherein service firms take over management of noncore business functions such as purchasing or accounts payable. Web-based applications have made it increasingly easy to outsource this work as well as manage it remotely. Oracle, HP, and Dell are a few of the hardware and software firms following the lead of IBM Global Services by beefing up their consulting services. As one consultant says, "The large hardware manufacturers know that their traditional core businesses have become little more than commodity businesses and that the real value is in services. Consulting services are a perfect complement to hardware and software sales. Manufacturers not only benefit from higher margins with consulting services, but they can also build their hardware sales through an enlarged relationship base."

Picking and Choosing

Every consulting firm will tell you that it stands out from the crowd: "We actually do implementation," "We make change happen," "We don't provide cookie-cutter solutions," or everybody's favorite, "It's our people that make us different." The reality is that most of the big firms are relatively similar, but we suggest that you avoid expressing this notion during your interviews. Consulting firms have a set of practices and cultural sensibilities that distinguish them from their competitors in nuanced ways, and they want you to pick up on those nuances. As you go through the interview process and, more important, as you seek a good match for yourself, look at the things that make the firms different. To give you a head start on that process, we've put together a simple guide that will help you distinguish one firm from another when you're out in the field (or in the interview cubicle).

THE PRACTICE ANGLE

Most consulting firms' marketing pitches reveal a constant tension between two competing messages: "We're specialized" (and therefore different from our competitors)

If you pull a consultant aside, buy him or her a few drinks, and refuse to accept a slippery answer, you might be able to squeeze out a carefully worded admission: Most firms do have a primary focus.

versus "We do everything" (so there's nothing our competitors do that we can't do better). Nevertheless, if you pull a consultant aside, buy him or her a few drinks, and refuse to accept a slippery answer, you might be able to squeeze out a carefully worded admission: Most firms do have a primary focus. McKinsey, Bain, and BCG are known for their strategy work. Booz Allen is particularly strong in organizational work. Accenture has traditionally had a strong information technology and systems focus.

THE JOB ANGLE

Other differences between firms include how many projects you work on at once, how formal the project team hierarchy is, how much the firm integrates client staff as team members, and where most of the work is done. These are all things you'll want to learn as you go through the interview process—they can have a significant impact on your day-to-day life. Both Bain and BCG typically require their consultants to take on two projects at once, whereas many other firms assign consultants only one project at a time. Bain and BCG also value face time with the client less than A.T. Kearney, Booz Allen, and Mercer do.

THE ATTITUDE ANGLE

Much of each consulting firm's recruiting and publicity resources go toward convincing candidates that "our firm has the best attitude in the business." For Bain, this means a strong emphasis on its youthful culture and company traditions like the Bain Band. For McKinsey, it means that consultants dress casually (well, sort of) for company information sessions. Any assessment of a firm's attitude is highly subjective. You'll want to develop your own sense of a firm's culture and lifestyle—and how you fit in with it—through your interactions with recruiters and staff.

ALL THE REST

Many other factors differentiate consulting firms. How international is it? What is its appraisal system? What are its levels of seniority? How much attention does it pay to diversity issues? What is its attitude toward balancing work and life? What is its growth curve? To help you get a better sense of how different firms answer these questions, we've included brief profiles in the next section. In addition, you may wish to see WetFeet's company-specific Insider Guides for extensive inside information about select firms. (See www.wetfeet.com.)

The Firms

Profiles of Major Players

Mini-Profiles

Note: The information on the following firms comes from firm websites, published articles, and WetFeet research. We've done our best to provide accurate information, but due to variations in reporting, changes due to market conditions, available information, and human error, there may be some discrepancies with actual numbers.

Profiles of Major Players

ACCENTURE

Primary U.S. Office:
1345 Avenue of the Americas
New York, NY 10105
Phone: 917-452-4400
Fax: 917-527-9915
www.accenture.com
Ticker: ACN

A consulting behemoth, Accenture—formerly Andersen Consulting—started out as the consulting sibling of tax and accounting firm Arthur Andersen. In 1999, tired of having to share profits with its poor relation, Andersen Consulting asked for its independence. Arthur Andersen refused, and the case was submitted to an international arbitration court. The arbitrator put much of the blame for the split on Arthur Andersen, and ordered Andersen Consulting to give up its name and pay $1 billion in exchange for its independence, significantly less than the $14 billion Arthur Andersen wanted. In 2001, Accenture spent $175 million to reintroduce itself under its new name and went public (the name rhymes with "adventure" and was meant to convey the firm's "accent on the future"). The timing couldn't have been more fortuitous—Arthur Andersen imploded in the wake of the Enron scandal shortly afterward.

Accenture offers management consulting, technology services, and outsourcing through five operating groups with 17 total industry groups. Led by CEO William Green, Accenture serves clients in every major industry around the world through 110 offices across 48 countries. In 2006, the firm acquired Savista, increasing its reach into middle-market business process outsourcing projects. Outsourcing was a particular area of strength in 2005, with revenues up 18 percent in U.S. dollars.

The Inside Scoop

"[Accenture] does more work behind the scenes, actually helping the client—not just creating more work for ourselves. We've even advised clients to hire competing vendors."

"Supervisors take an active interest in whether you're becoming better at business, and in your technical and industry knowledge."

Key Facts

- In 2005, Accenture's practice in Europe/Middle East/Africa grew 19 percent and its Asia Pacific practice grew 14 percent. Its Americas practice grew 8 percent.

- Accenture (which is based in Bermuda to avoid U.S. income tax) runs the Internal Revenue Service's website.

- Has around 4,100 senior executives.

Key Financial Stats

2005 revenue: $15,547 million
1-year growth rate: 15 percent

Personnel Highlights

Number of consultants: 129,000
1-year growth rate: 15 percent

Buy the WetFeet Insider Guide on Accenture for more information about the firm.

THE ADVISORY BOARD COMPANY

2445 M Street, NW
Washington, DC 20037
Phone: 202-266-5600
Fax: 202-266-5700
www.advisoryboardcompany.com
Ticker: ABCO

The Advisory Board Company falls somewhere between a consulting firm, a think tank, and a publisher, providing syndicated and customized research along with daily news to member organizations on best practices in the field of health care. It hires undergraduates, MBAs, and advanced-degree candidates to research issues of concern to its membership, and it pays close attention to the written and visual expression and presentation of its research results.

Founded in 1979, the Advisory Board counted half of the Fortune 500 as clients after 18 months. It split off its corporate research offerings into the Corporate Executive Board in 1999. In 2000, it started offering shorter, more frequent publications and began offering its research online, through its website. It also created H*Works, a workforce that collaborates with hospitals and health-care systems to improve performance through application of Advisory Board research. In late 2001, the firm went public.

Today, some 2,500 hospitals, health systems, pharmaceutical and biotech companies, health-care insurers, and medical device companies are members. In 2006, the Advisory Board launched the Surgery Performance program to help Chief Operating Officers improve performance of the surgery department, with charter members including the University of Texas Medical Branch Hospitals and Clarian Health Partners.

The Inside Scoop

"My learning curve is always vertical. I'm in way over my head all the time."

Key Facts

- Publishes 50 major studies and 3,000 customized research briefs a year.

- Specializes in research for health-care organizations; the average study surveys 2,000 pages of literature and requires 100-plus interviews, and captures 10 to 20 business or clinical practices.

- Unlike other consulting firms, the Advisory Board focuses on helping clients think through broad trends in an entire industry's structure and direction.

Key Financial Stats

2005 revenue: $159.1 million
1-year growth rate: 12 percent

Personnel Highlights

Number of employees: 750
1-year growth rate: 30 percent

A.T. KEARNEY, INC.

222 West Adams Street
Chicago, IL 60606
Phone: 312-648-0111
Fax: 312-223-6200
www.atkearney.com

A.T. Kearney founder Andrew Thomas Kearney was J.O. McKinsey's (of McKinsey & Company fame) first partner. The firm took its current name in 1946, though its predecessor firm was started in 1926. It competed with the elite strategy firms, offering strategy, operations, and technology consulting. In 1995, computer services firm EDS acquired A.T. Kearney. However, the acquisition did not go well, due in part to bankruptcies at major EDS clients WorldCom and US Airways, an SEC investigation, earnings shortfalls at EDS, and declining revenues at A.T. Kearney. EDS CEO Michael Jordan, who took over in 2003, restored Kearney's independence and reorganized its management, but revenues at Kearney continued to fall. In 2005, EDS tried to sell Kearney to the Monitor Group, but when those talks fell through A.T. Kearney instead celebrated its 80th year (2006) with a management buyout, which involved 170 A.T. Kearney officers from 26 countries. This makes A.T. Kearney, once again, an independent, privately owned management consultancy; EDS remains a client of the firm. A.T. Kearney's primary governance vehicle is an 11-member board of directors elected by the A.T. Kearney officers.

The firm expects to pursue the same opportunities as it did while it was part of EDS, and thinks that its model makes its shareholders more entrepreneurial—which it hopes will lead to more work. Scuttlebutt on the buyout priced it at $250,000 to $400,000 per shareholder, according to a *Consultants News* report, with more demand than shares available. The firm's campus recruiting is reported to be among the most competitive in years, but with a high acceptance rate—and even some alumni returning. The firm operates in 30 countries.

Key Facts

- Organized into both industry and business practice groups.

- Firm surveys showed 98.4 percent of clients rating performance as excellent or good in 2005.

- The firm publishes *Executive Agenda*; PDFs of articles are available online at the company's website.

Key Financial Stats

Not available

Personnel Highlights

Number of consultants: 3,000
1-year growth rate: 0 percent

To find out how A.T. Kearney describes itself, check out the free Recruiter Q&A at www.wetfeet.com.

BAIN & COMPANY, INC.

131 Dartmouth Street
Boston, MA 02116
Phone: 617-572-2000
Fax: 617-572-2427
www.bain.com

Bain & Company is a leading strategy consulting firm with 32 offices around the world. It provides strategic advice and recommended solutions to business problems to leading companies in virtually every economic sector. Bain was founded in 1973 by Bill Bain, a former VP at the Boston Consulting Group, and several others. In the beginning, Bain distinguished itself by forging long-term relationships with clients by agreeing not to work with their competitors in exchange for reciprocal fidelity. Bain's capabilities include strategy, customer and product management, growth, organization, supply chain management, cost and capital management, M&A, core process redesign, and private equity.

The firm—as well as its clients—has performed particularly well over the last ten years (see the stock chart on its homepage). In 2004, Bain director and global strategy practice leader Chris Zook's *Beyond the Core*—which focuses on how companies can grow profitably by focusing on their core business—came out; in 2006, the founder of Bain's Loyalty practice, Fred Reichheld, published *The Ultimate Question*, which explores how companies can increase customer, employee, partner, and investor loyalty.

The Inside Scoop

"I think of Bain as more street-smart and entrepreneurial."

"We're data-driven, but we're also very thought-driven. Asserting new ideas is just as important as backing up your ideas with research."

Key Facts

- Strong culture—there is definitely a Bain way of doing things.

- Consultants and associate consultants are often staffed on two projects at once.

- The Bridgespan Group is a nonprofit launched by Bain to bring strategic consulting to the nonprofit sector.

Key Financial Stats

Not available

Personnel Highlights

Number of consultants: 2,400
1-year growth rate: 8 percent

Buy the WetFeet Insider Guide on Bain & Company for more information about the firm. And to find out how Bain describes itself, check out the free Recruiter Q&A at www.wetfeet.com.

BEARINGPOINT, INC.

1676 International Drive
McLean, VA 22102
Phone: 703-747-3000 or 866-276-4768 (toll-free)
Fax: 703-747-8500
www.bearingpoint.com
Ticker: BE

BearingPoint, formerly known as KPMG Consulting, is a system integrator and business adviser. The firm's three industry groups—Public Services, Commercial Services, and Financial Services—provide solutions to clients of all sizes, and are augmented by alliances with technology companies like Cisco Systems, Microsoft, Oracle, and SAP. The firm traces its roots to 1870, when William Barclay Peat (the P in the former KPMG moniker) founded his London accounting firm. More than a century of mergers culminated in 1987, when Peat Marwick International and Klynveld Main Goerdeler merged to become a modern, world-class firm. The consulting arm separated from KPMG, its Big Four (then Big Five) parent, in 2000. In 2001, BearingPoint/KPMG went public, and in 2002 it changed its name to BearingPoint. It also went on an acquisition spree, adding 17 practices, including KPMG Consulting AG in Germany and the practices of Andersen Business Consulting in Australia, Brazil, China, France, and many other countries. Today, the firm has offices in 39 countries.

In mid-2005, business appeared good, but financial controls were not: the firm reported to the SEC that it didn't know when it would be able to report 2004 financial results and cautioned that results dating back to 2002 might be inaccurate. The firm hired Harry L. You, former CFO of Oracle, as its CEO in March 2005 as part of a gambit to win back investor confidence, but a year later it put off reporting 2005 results.

In April 2006, BearingPoint replaced its India Global Development Center with a bigger, newer facility, complementing its China Global Development Center in offering software development and IT services.

The Inside Scoop

"People are competitive with themselves, but not with each other."

Key Facts

- Plans to close unprofitable offices in some countries and expand in China and India.

- Clients include all 15 Cabinet-level departments of the U.S. federal government, the top 10 banking and finance companies in the United States, and all 13 global pharmaceutical companies.

- First among the Big Five to separate its consulting business from auditing—and the first Big Five consulting practice to go public.

Key Financial Stats

Not available*

* BearingPoint postponed filing 2005 results, and has not filed quarterly financial results with the SEC since the third quarter of 2004. S&P projects gross margins in the 13 to 14 percent range in 2005 and 2006. Estimates on most recently available information as of May 2005, based on S&P projections. Revenues for 2004 were $3,376 million.

Personnel Highlights

Number of consultants: 16,800
1-year growth rate: 5 percent

BOOZ ALLEN HAMILTON

Corporate Headquarters:
8283 Greensboro Drive
McLean, VA 22102
Phone: 703-902-5000
Fax: 703-902-3333
www.boozallen.com

Worldwide Commercial Business:
101 Park Avenue
New York, NY 10178
Phone: 212-697-1900
Fax: 212-551-6732

Founded in 1914, Booz Allen Hamilton is one of the oldest and most respected firms in the consulting industry. With more than 100 offices on six continents, it's a major force domestically and internationally. Up until this year, the firm comprised two business units: the Worldwide Commercial Business (WCB) and the considerably larger Worldwide Technology Business (WTB). But in April 2006 the firm merged them into one massive unit in a sweeping move titled the "one firm evolution." Booz Allen traditionally catered to Fortune 1000 companies, competing with strategy consulting firms like McKinsey, Bain, and BCG, while its large-scale implementation projects have made it comparable to firms like Accenture and government-consulting powerhouse SAIC. Booz Allen is now focusing on leveraging its strengths across the entire firm by creating mixed teams with skills drawn from various parts of the firm.

Booz Allen's track record of serving both private- and public-sector clients is certainly its strongest differentiator, but as a result the company is sometimes viewed—by both insiders and outsiders—as two firms within a firm. A companywide rebranding effort was launched in 2001 to position Booz Allen as one firm serving both public- and private-sector clients, and it succeeded in alleviating to some degree that perception in the consulting marketplace.

In 2006, Booz was awarded a ten-year contract from the U.S. Army to provide support to command, control, communication, computer, intelligence, surveillance, and recon systems, and it has been hiring aggressively in Virginia for homeland-security-related jobs.

The Inside Scoop

"Titles don't matter. Here I'm a senior consultant; at another firm I'd be an associate. You could call me 'elephant' and I'd still be doing the same thing."

"The Booz Allen culture is cooperative rather than competitive, and people routinely share information with others."

Key Facts

- According to a Department of Defense press advisory, Booz Allen is one of the "100 Companies Receiving the Largest Dollar Volume of Prime Contract Awards— Fiscal Year 2005," ranking 15th among Air Force Contractors, 25th among Navy Contractors, and 47th among the Army contractors.

- Booz was the number one ranked company for its employee-sponsored workforce training and development in *Training Magazine*'s 2006 "Top 100 list."

- Clients include the government of Greece, for which Booz Allen helped manage the transportation for the Athens Olympics, and the National Security Agency, for whom Booz Allen is the biggest contractor.

Key Financial Stats

2005 revenue: $3,500 million

1-year growth rate: 6 percent

Personnel Highlights

Number of employees: 17,000

1-year growth rate: 6 percent

Buy the WetFeet Insider Guide on Booz Allen Hamilton for more information about the company. And to find out how Booz Allen describes itself, check out the free Recruiter Q&A at www.wetfeet.com.

THE BOSTON CONSULTING GROUP

Exchange Place, 31st Floor
Boston, MA 02109
Phone: 617-973-1200
Fax: 617-973-1399
www.bcg.com

The Boston Consulting Group is one of the top-tier management consulting firms. Founded in 1963, BCG came to prominence in the 1970s when it began challenging McKinsey & Company for high-level strategy work with large corporations. The firm has developed a number of analytical tools, such as capability-driven competitive strategies, and concepts, such as total shareholder return, that are used throughout the consulting industry. BCG has always had a strong international presence; the second office it opened is in Tokyo.

In 2006, insiders report that BCG's growth has been very strong, with high utilization rates. In 2005, the firm hired a large class, but the class of 2006 was the largest in BCG's history, and insiders tell us the firm has brought in senior-level hires to balance out the pyramid. The firm has 60 offices in 36 countries.

The Inside Scoop

"The impact you have on clients, irrespective of your title, can be huge."

"There's a BCG thought process, but no template—it's not canned. I think it lets us be a little more innovative."

Key Facts

*   Heavier focus on strategy and operations projects than other firms.

*   Arguably one of the most prestigious consulting firms in the world.

*   Named to *Fortune*'s annual "100 Best Companies to Work For" list, placing 11th overall and 3rd among smaller companies.

Key Financial Stats

2005 revenue: $1,500 million

1-year growth rate: 13 percent

Personnel Highlights

Number of consultants: 2,900

1-year growth rate: 10 percent

Buy the WetFeet Insider Guide on BCG for more information about the company.

CAPGEMINI

Place de l'Etoile
11 rue de Tilsitt
75017 Paris, France
Phone: +33-1-47-54-50-00
Fax: +33-1-42-27-32-11
www.capgemini.com

U.S. Headquarters:
750 Seventh Avenue, Suite 1800
New York, NY 10019
Phone: 212-314-8000
Fax: 212-314-8001

Capgemini, the largest supplier of information technology services in Europe, became the world's second-largest consulting practice when it acquired the management consulting side of Ernst & Young in May 2000. The combined entity is structured into four business lines: consulting, technology services, outsourcing, and local professional services. Sogeti, a wholly owned subsidiary of Capgemini, provides information technology services to businesses and public sector organizations.

By acquiring Ernst & Young, Capgemini significantly increased its North American business just a few weeks before the Internet bubble burst. At the time, the acquisition seemed like the melding of complementary strengths in information systems integration, but it soon turned sour, and the firm is still recovering. After multiple years of revenue declines, Capgemini announced in May 2005 a reorganization that involved closing nearly half of its 40 North American offices. Entering 2006, the firm was profitable in regions outside North America, and had gained positive margins in its North American business. But high levels of attrition—during a competitive recruiting period—have led some to wonder about the firm's ability to compete effectively in North America. Keep an eye on 2006 results to see how the firm's Map Initiative, a plan to improve profitability through outsourcing, is working.

Key Facts

- Capgemini stock is publicly traded on the Euronext Paris, but not in the United States.

- On April 2004, the firm changed its name to Capgemini, dropping Ernst & Young, as part of its rebranding campaign.

- The local professional services business was up 8 percent in 2005 over 2004 results, and revenue rose in excess of 10 percent.

Key Financial Stats

2005 revenue (in euros): €6,954 million

1-year growth rate: 10 percent

Personnel Highlights

Number of employees: 60,000

1-year growth rate: 1 percent

CGI GROUP

1130 Sherbrooke Street West, Fifth Floor
Montreal, Quebec H3A 2M8
Canada
Phone: 514-841-3200
or 800-637-3799 (toll-free)
Fax: 514-841-3299
www.cgi.com
Ticker: GIB

U.S. Headquarters:
4050 Legato Road
Fairfax, VA 22033
Phone: 703-267-8000
Fax: 703-267-5111

CGI Group is the largest Canadian IT services firm, offering end-to-end IT and business process outsourcing services. Founded in 1976, CGI is 30 percent owned by Bell Canada Enterprises, Canada's biggest telecom group. CGI has grown rapidly over the last several years via acquisitions—averaging more than five a year since 2000—and through its strong telecommunications and financial services practices. In May 2004, it acquired American Management Systems (AMS), adding 5,000 employees and making CGI Group one of the world's ten largest computer consulting firms. The acquisition also made CGI Group a player in public services; AMS does half its business with federal, state, and local governments. AMS, based in Fairfax, Virginia, was founded by four former Pentagon employees in 1970, went public in 1979, and targeted government, financial services, and the communications, media, and entertainment industries for its enterprise integration, managed services, and innovation and transformation services. The strategy seems to be working: The Commonwealth of Virginia, the State of Utah, and San Bernardino County, California, all have signed contracts with CGI-AMS since the acquisition.

Key Facts

- CGI founders Serge Godin and André Imbeau continue to run the company as executive chairman of the board and executive vice president and CFO, respectively.

- CGI calls its employees *members*, not employees, but that didn't stop it from announcing in March 2006 that it would eliminate 1,000 positions in order to strengthen its competitive position.

Key Financial Stats

2005 revenue: $3,685 million

1-year growth rate: 18 percent

Personnel Highlights

Number of employees: 25,000

1-year growth rate: 0 percent

COMPUTER SCIENCES CORPORATION

2100 E. Grand Avenue
El Segundo, CA 90245
Phone: 310-615-0311
Fax: 310-322-9768
www.csc.com
Ticker: CSC

Computer Sciences Corporation (CSC) provides IT services to U.S. government agencies, including the Department of Defense, and corporations such as DuPont, Merrill Lynch, and Visa. Founded in 1959 with $100 and a contract from Honeywell to develop a business language compiler, it is today one of the largest computer services companies in the U.S. government market. The company provides a broad spectrum of services to its clients, including business strategy, change management, and value-added solutions for the chemical and energy industries, such as management consulting, systems integration, and outsourcing. It has a strong systems integration practice and strategic alliances with major firms including IBM, HP, SAP, and Oracle. The company operates in more than 80 countries.

At the close of 2005, CSC reported a pipeline of $28 billion in federal work through 2007, spread over some 390 programs. Utilization and billing rates were also on the rise, though there had been a decline in revenues from European operations.

Key Facts

- Cofounder Roy Nutt was a member of the IBM team that developed FORTRAN.

- CSC provides business consulting and IT services to the U.S. Postal Service.

- Outsourcing made up 46 percent of revenue, and IT and professional services 54 percent, for the first nine months of fiscal 2006.

Key Financial Stats

2005 consulting revenue: $14,610 million

1-year growth rate: 4 percent

Personnel Highlights

Number of employees: 80,000

1-year growth rate: 1 percent

THE CORPORATE EXECUTIVE BOARD COMPANY

2000 Pennsylvania Avenue, NW
Suite 6000
Washington, DC 20006
Phone: 202-777-5000
Fax: 202-777-5100
www.executiveboard.com
Ticker: EXBD

The Corporate Executive Board was born in 1993 as the corporate practice of the Advisory Board Company, and in 1999 it spun out in an IPO. The Corporate Executive Board provides best-practice information to businesses, specializing in strategy, operations, and general management issues. It operates on a membership model, in which it delivers functional and industry-specific research and education to senior executives at more than 2,800 member companies. Companies join to gain access to cutting-edge research in the form of complex research studies, short-answer research on specific issues customized to members, onsite education and training, and networking opportunities with other members. The company has offices in Washington, D.C., and London.

In 2006, the Corporate Executive Board plans to launch five to six new programs. The first of these is the Project Management Executive Council, designed to serve senior IT executives who manage IT projects at large companies.

Key Facts

- Offers a program called ServiceCorps, which brings employees together in teams to serve the local community through volunteering.

- Conducts more than 40,000 interviews every year with executives, managers, consultants, and economists across 30 distinct research programs.

- Client renewal rate was 92 percent in 2005.

Key Financial Stats

2005 revenue: $362.2 million

1-year growth rate: 29 percent

Personnel Highlights

Number of consultants: 1,865

1-year growth rate: 20 percent

DELOITTE CONSULTING

25 Broadway
New York, NY 10004
Phone: 212-618-4000
Fax: 212-618-4500
www.deloitte.com

Deloitte Consulting is part of the global professional services organization Deloitte Touche Tohmatsu International. The firm offers its clients a selection of service lines that include enterprise applications, human capital, outsourcing, strategy and operations, and technology integration. It focuses on nine industries: aviation and transport services; consumer business; energy and resources; financial services; life sciences and health care; manufacturing; public sector; real estate; and technology, media, and communications. It ranks among the top five consulting practices in North America in terms of revenue.

Deloitte has a reputation for being less aggressive than many other firms, but that doesn't come at the expense of prestige—it's among only six firms (Bain, McKinsey, Booz, BCG, and A.T.. Kearney are the other five) that are recognized by at least 85 percent of MBAs, according to a *Consultants News* report. Like its Big Four rivals, Deloitte considered spinning off its high-end strategy consulting unit under the name Braxton; unlike its rivals, however, it kept consulting as part of the audit firm, abandoning those plans in 2003. The firm is particularly strong in work-life balance compared to many of its peers.

The Inside Scoop

"There are a lot of partners who welcome you walking into their office or giving them a call."

Key Facts

- In 2005, Deloitte was named to *Working Mother*'s "100 Best Companies for Working Mothers" list for the 12th consecutive year; among its benefits, Deloitte offers 24 weeks of job-guaranteed maternity leave—eight of those weeks with full salary for new moms.

- *Training* magazine ranked Deloitte sixth on its 2005 list of the "Top 100" companies for training.

- Deloitte Touche Tohmatsu is a founding member of the UN's Global Compact, which promotes responsible global citizenship and advances universal values in business around the world.

Key Financial Stats

2005 revenue (consulting): $4,300 million

1-year growth rate: 7 percent

Personnel Highlights

Number of employees: 120,000 (includes consulting, tax, audit, and financial advisory)

1-year growth rate: 4 percent

DIAMONDCLUSTER INTERNATIONAL, INC.

The John Hancock Center
875 N. Michigan Avenue, Suite 3000
Chicago, IL 60611
Phone: 312-255-5000
Fax: 312-255-6000
www.diamondcluster.com
Ticker: DTPI

DiamondCluster International was formed in 2000 when Cluster Consulting and Diamond Technology Partners merged. Cluster, which was founded in 1993, was more international; Diamond Technology Partners, founded in 1994, was known for its use of small interdisciplinary teams and its virtual office structure. The firm works with companies to help them effectively employ emerging technologies. The firm serves Global 2000 clients and has offices in North America, Europe, the Middle East, India, and Latin America. It also operates the DiamondExchange, a program that facilitates conversations among top executives and experts in strategy, technology, operations, and learning.

After a serious drop-off in business following the dotcom bust, the firm is back on track, with strong fiscal years in both 2004 and 2005—including double-digit revenue growth. Fiscal 2006 results are not looking as robust as the previous two years, but the firm anticipates double-digit growth in 2007. DiamondCluster's newest offices are in Dubai and Mumbai, India, reflecting its broadening geographic reach. Adam Gutstein took over as CEO in April 2006.

Key Facts

- During the third quarter of 2006, revenue per consultant was $331,000.

- The firm has been purchasing stock at an average rate of one million shares a quarter.

- DTPI is the company's stock symbol as well as an acronym for the qualities to which the company aspires: discipline, talent, partnering, and intellectual capital.

Key Financial Stats

2005 revenue: $193 million
1-year growth rate: 8 percent

Personnel Highlights

Number of consultants: 751
1-year growth rate: 24 percent

IBM GLOBAL SERVICES

1 New Orchard Road
Armonk, NY 10504
Phone: 914-499-1900
Fax: 914-765-7382
www-1.ibm.com/services
Ticker (parent company): IBM

IBM may be better known for its computer hardware, but Big Blue's largest division is Global Services, which competes with the likes of Accenture, EDS, and HP Technology Services. Originally, IBM ran a consulting unit under the name IBM Consulting, but in 2000, it merged that group with its systems integration group to provide end-to-end business solutions. In 2002, IBM acquired PricewaterhouseCoopers (PwC), a 30,000-person firm that traced its lineage back to Price Waterhouse and Coopers & Lybrand. PwC brought a client roster that included about 45 percent of the Fortune 500; higher-margin consulting skills; and experience in financial services, government, and consumer products that expanded IBM Global Service's expertise and capabilities. Created in 1991, IBM Global Services has since grown to account for 35 percent of IBM's revenue in 2005, making it one of the world's largest consulting services organizations.

Today, IBM uses its size to win business transformation and outsourcing engagements. Business transformation—or, rather, Business Performance Transformation Services, which offers support on things like supply chain, human resources, and logistics—saw revenue increase 28 percent in 2005, to $4 billion.

The Inside Scoop

"I didn't have much of a technical background when I joined the firm, but [my training] changed that."

"[The firm] has deep pockets and is able to afford training and knowledge databases that a lot of smaller firms can't. It makes my life easier."

"One thing I've noticed, I'm working with extraordinarily nice people. A lot of firms are cut-throat and high pressure, but people here are really nice and supportive. It's a mentorship culture; they're really interested in helping you develop and grow."

Key Facts

- New recruits go through IBM Global Services Institute, where IBM professionals teach them the ropes.

- Has alliances with Cisco, Oracle, SAP, and Siebel Systems, among others.

- Reported a backlog of $111 billion in projects at the end of 2005.

Key Financial Stats

2005 revenue: $47,400 million
1-year growth rate: 2 percent

Personnel Highlights

Number of employees: 190,000
1-year growth rate: 0 percent

L.E.K. CONSULTING

40 Grosvenor Place
London SW1X 7JL
United Kingdom
Phone: +44-020-7389-7200
Fax: +44-020-7389-7440
www.lek.com

U.S. Headquarters:
28 State Street, 16th Floor
Boston, MA 02109
Phone: 617-951-9500
Fax: 617-951-9392

L.E.K. Consulting was founded in 1983 and has since advised 20 percent of the largest companies in the United States, Europe, Asia, and Australia. It works with companies on prioritizing business opportunities, entering new markets, improving performance, and evaluating acquisitions around the world. L.E.K. Consulting divides its expertise into three principal areas: business strategy, shareholder value, and mergers and acquisitions. It emphasizes research and analysis to make data-driven recommendations and targets the midmarket in many of its practice areas. About a third of its business is in M&A.

The firm offers consultants an opportunity for rapid career growth—three quarters of its current partners were consultants with the firm, and a third of these consultants were associates with the firm—and is decentralized, with partners taking responsibility for developing their own businesses. L.E.K. has 16 offices in 11 countries.

Key Facts

- Founded in London in 1983 by three former Bain & Company partners, the firm considers itself more global in its thinking than U.S.-focused firms.

- Partners spend 70 percent of their time working with consultants and associates; the average case team consists of eight professionals.

- A recognized leader in the area of shareholder value, the firm is known for its "Shareholder Scoreboard," published annually in the *Wall Street Journal*.

Key Financial Stats

Not available

Personnel Highlights

Number of employees: 500
1-year growth rate: 10 percent

MARAKON ASSOCIATES

245 Park Avenue, 44th Floor
New York, NY 10167
Phone: 212-377-5000
Fax: 212-377-6000
www.marakon.com

Three former corporate finance executives from Wells Fargo Bank and one academic formed Marakon Associates in 1978. Two of the four founders remain today; Paul Kontes, a third, retired in March 2005 after 25 years, and remains involved as chairman emeritus. A small firm, with six and a half consultants per partner, Marakon assists CEOs and other top management with strategy and organization. The firm is known for "values-based management," which is all about maximizing shareholder value for client businesses. While that concept may seem clichéd today, it was a pioneering idea when the firm was founded in 1978. It also makes the firm plenty of money: Marakon regularly ranks among the top U.S. consultancies in revenue per consultant, even though the firm is still relatively unknown despite its age, pedigree, and impressive growth. About half of its clients are in the financial services sector.

Marakon requires all consultants, regardless of seniority, to spend a significant part of their time working with clients. The company has five offices, including three in the United States and one each in London and Singapore.

Key Facts

- After a year at the firm, all employees can take up to two months of unpaid leave a year, as well as a three-month sabbatical every two years.

- Employees get 200 hours of formal training in their first 15 months.

- Benefits include 12 weeks of paid maternity leave.

Key Financial Stats

Not available

Personnel Highlights

Number of employees: 300
1-year growth rate: 0 percent

To find out how Marakon Associates describes itself, check out the free Recruiter Q&A at www.wetfeet.com.

MCKINSEY & COMPANY

55 E. 52nd Street, 21st Floor
New York, NY 10022
Phone: 212-446-7000
Fax: 212-446-8575
www.mckinsey.com

McKinsey & Company is perhaps the most famous consulting firm in the world, with a long history of providing strategic advice to the top management of the world's largest corporations. McKinsey was founded in 1926 when James O. McKinsey teamed up with partner Andrew T. Kearney to form a business advisory service. They were later joined by Marvin Bower, a Harvard MBA who went on to actively manage the firm for more than 30 years. McKinsey is renowned for its strict business standards, its strong culture, and for the breadth and depth of its experience base; it's also known to charge among the highest fees for its work. Among consultants, McKinsey is the gold standard by which reputation and success are measured.

From 1994 to 2001, the firm more than doubled in number of consultants and revenue. Struggles followed: in 2003, some associates reported that the road to partner status had lengthened; three practice leaders were hired away between November 2004 and April 2005; and in late 2005 there were reports of more unsolicited McKinsey resumes going to recruiters. But don't count the firm out yet: McKinsey continues to be the number one place MBAs want to work in the 2006 Universum poll. It is currently bolstering newly launched practices, such as its technology office, and practices in nontraditional geographies, while hiring more seasoned veterans. It also has a strong record of hiring PhDs and medical doctors. McKinsey has 80 offices in 44 countries.

The Inside Scoop

"The people here are the biggest draw. They're smart, and they have a respect for the integrity of ideas. Even if you're the most junior person on a team, if you come up with a good idea, it will be respected."

"The lifestyle is always a challenge. It's always [the] client first, and it's a bummer to check your voicemail at nine o'clock at night and realize there's something you have to do before the morning. If you let it, work will consume you."

Key Facts

- Famous for its strong network and strong culture.

- About half of the firm's graduate school hires are MBAs; the other half come from PhD and medical programs.

- Hiring in Asia rose from 15 to 20 percent of overall firm totals.

- A midlevel associate responsible for managing a single client costs around $2,500 a day.

Key Financial Stats

Not available

Personnel Highlights

Not available

Buy the WetFeet Insider Guide on McKinsey for more information about the firm.

MERCER MANAGEMENT CONSULTING, INC.

1166 Avenue of the Americas, 32nd Floor
New York, NY 10036
Phone: 212-345-8000
Fax: 217-345-8075
www.mercermc.com

Mercer Management Consulting was born in 1992, when parent company Marsh & McLennan merged two of its consulting subsidiaries, Temple Barker & Sloane and Strategic Planning Associates. Today, it is one of seven consulting arms of Mercer Inc. (see "Mini-Profiles"), focusing on growth and strategy. An aspiring top-tier strategy consultancy, the firm seems particularly proud of its "thought leadership"; eight books have been published by its consultants since 1995, the most recent of which is Adrian Slywotzky's *How to Grow When Markets Don't*, which came out in 2003. (In 2004, sibling Mercer Human Resource Consulting came out with *Play to Your Strengths*.) The firm's capabilities—business strategy, brand strategy and identity consulting, and operations—are targeted to growing shareholder value.

In 2003, Oliver, Wyman & Company merged with Mercer's financial services strategy and risk consulting units to deliver financial services strategy and risk management consulting. In 2004, Mercer acquired Spanish firm C.R.M. Concord, a Madrid-based strategy and operations consulting firm. And in 2006, Mercer acquired MultiModal Applied Systems, which consults on railway systems planning and service design software. The firm has 24 offices around the world.

The Inside Scoop

"I had some offers from more reputable, brand-name firms, but I just really liked the people and the culture of Mercer."

"Partners have a real incentive to mentor you and give you the insight to get promoted and move on to the next level."

Key Facts

- Less structure and more low-key attitude than other leading firms.

- Draws on expertise of others in the Mercer Specialty Consulting unit, such as financial services from Mercer Oliver Wyman and change management consulting from Mercer Delta.

- Offers its consultants externships—6 to 24 months working for a client, startup, nonprofit, or other organization.

Key Financial Stats

2005 revenue: $909 million (Mercer Specialty Consulting; includes Mercer Management Consulting, Mercer Oliver Wyman, Mercer Delta Organizational Consulting, NERA Economic Consulting, and Lippincott Mercer)
1-year growth rate: 17 percent

Personnel Highlights

Number of employees: 1,000
1-year growth rate: –37 percent

THE MONITOR GROUP

2 Canal Park
Cambridge, MA 02141
Phone: 617-252-2000
Fax: 617-252-2100
www.monitor.com

Monitor Company Group was formed in 1983 by Harvard Business School professor Mark Fuller, his brother Joe, and five other HBS graduates who wanted to create a better strategy-focused consulting firm. It quickly earned a seat at the table of the consulting elite. Today, it calls itself The Monitor Group, and is organized into three business units—Monitor Action Group, Monitor Merchant Banking, and the Intelligent Products Group. Each business group is further subdivided into "group companies." The strategy consultants are in the Action Group; while the Intelligent Products Group, consisting of Monitor Software, provides custom software and information systems. Monitor Merchant Banking includes Monitor Clipper Partners, which invests in middle-market companies, primarily through leveraged buyouts; Monitor Ventures, which provides capital and services to technology companies; and three other groups. The Monitor Action Company (called the Action Company) is the firm's largest and oldest operation. It goes head-to-head with McKinsey and the Boston Consulting Group and wins top-level strategy assignments from Fortune 500 clients.

A little less than a quarter of the firm's work is competitive strategy, with more than 40 percent in the area of marketing and growth strategy. Geographically, around 70 percent of the firm's work is in North America and Europe, split fairly evenly between the two. Health care is its biggest practice area, followed by telecommunications/computing, consumer products, and financial services. The firm has 28 offices.

The Inside Scoop

"I like the fact that if I'm willing and able, I can enter into some interesting roles in managing clients or making presentations. Monitor is very eager to have people progress—to give them opportunities."

"The company's flexibility and willingness to let people make individual choices generate incredible loyalty and better performance from people."

Key Facts

- Innovative recruiting, compensation, and career advancement policies.

- More than 55 percent of its revenue comes from clients it has been serving continuously for three years or more.

- Does not release revenue information, but *Consultants News* puts growth in 2005 in the high teens.

Key Financial Stats

Not available

Personnel Highlights

Not available

To find out how Monitor Group describes itself, check out the free Recruiter Q&A at www.wetfeet.com.

NAVIGANT CONSULTING INC.

615 N. Wabash Avenue
Chicago, IL 60611
Phone: 312-573-5600
Fax: 312-573-5678
www.navigantconsulting.com
Ticker: NCI

Navigant is a global firm that serves Fortune 500 companies, government agencies, and law firms. Its consulting services include construction, corporate finance, discovery services, energy, financial insurance and claims services, government contracting, health care, and litigation and investigations focusing on industries undergoing regulatory or structural change. The company has grown through acquisition, having integrated Peterson Consulting, which advises on disputes, regulation, and change; PENTA Advisory Services, a financial consulting firm; Bookman-Edmonston, a water resources practice; Andersen's government contracts consulting practice; AD Little's Advanced Energy Systems Practice; and Tucker Alan, a privately held litigation and business-consulting firm. In 2005, it added five firms, including the 24-person Tiber Group, a strategy shop that consults for health-care executives, and the 23-person Casas, Benjamin & White, a financial advisory firm with particular strength in health care. Navigant Consulting has offices in more than 40 North American cities; three offices in China; and one office each in London and Prague.

Key Facts

- Formerly known as The Metzler Group.

- Growing by acquisition; added five companies in 2005.

- Don't mistake Navigant Consulting with Navigant International, the travel management services company (Navigant Consulting uses "Navigant" under license from Navigant International).

Key Financial Stats

2005 revenue: $576 million

1-year growth rate: 16 percent

Personnel Highlights

Number of consultants: 1,700

1-year growth rate: 9 percent

PITTIGLIO RABIN TODD & MCGRATH

1050 Winter Street, Suite 3000
Waltham, MA 02451
Phone: 781-647-2800
Fax: 781-647-2804
www.prtm.com

Founded in 1976, Pittiglio Rabin Todd & McGrath is a management consulting firm to the high-tech industry, focusing on strategy, operations and supply chain management, strategic IT management, marketing and sales, customer service and support, and product and technology development processes (which it calls *product and cycle-time excellence*, or PACE). It serves startups as well as multinationals.

Candidates interested in the firm might want to check out cofounder Michael McGrath's 2004 book, *Next Generation Product Development*; Shoshanah Cohen and Joseph Roussel's 2005 *Strategic Supply Chain Management*; and PRTM's *Insight*, which is published on the firm's website. Consultants can make partnership in seven to nine years. The firm has 14 offices in the United States, Europe, and Asia.

The Inside Scoop

"We're extremely collaborative. We're very team-oriented at the top level, and that has a trickle-down effect."

Key Facts

- Director/consultant ratio of 4:1.

- Flat organizational structure, with consultants working in small cross-functional teams.

- *Consulting Magazine* ranked PRTM among the "Top Ten Consulting Firms to Work For" in 2005—the fourth year in a row that the firm made the list.

Key Financial Stats

Not available

Personnel Highlights

Number of employees: 500
1-year growth rate: 20 percent

ROLAND BERGER STRATEGY CONSULTANTS GMBH

Arabellastrasse 33
81925 Munich
Germany
Phone: 49-89-9230-0
Fax: 49-89-9230-8202
www.rolandberger.com

U.S. Headquarters:
230 Park Avenue, Suite 112
New York, NY 10022
Phone: 212-651-9660
Fax: 212-756-8750

Roland Berger, which was founded in Germany in 1967, is a strategy firm with 32 offices in Europe, Asia, and the Americas. Wholly owned by about 130 partners, Roland Berger works with some 30 percent of the Global 1000 and more than 40 percent of Europe's leading companies. The firm offers services in corporate strategy and organization, information management, operations strategy, marketing and sales, and restructuring and corporate finance. Until 1998, it was part of Deutsche Bank, limiting the work it could do with financial service organizations. Financial services is now a growth sector for the firm. Roland Berger has U.S. offices in New York and Detroit.

New hires don't need to be explicit about the specific practice area in which they want to work, and will get help finding their way from management (whether they want it or not). The firm does not have deadlines for applicants and asks candidates for junior consultant or consultant positions to contact the firm four to nine months before finishing their studies. It invites candidates to apply through its online application form. In April 2006, it announced plans to hire 150 people over the next year.

Key Facts

- Roland Berger, the firm's founder, was born in 1937 and remained active in the firm as global managing partner and chairman of the executive committee until July 2003, when he moved to the supervisory board.

- The firm provides business advice in nearly 20 languages, and understands the nuances among European cultures.

Key Financial Stats

Not available

Personnel Highlights

Number of employees: 1,630
1-year growth rate: −4 percent

Mini-Profiles

The following mini-profiles provide information about boutique and specialized firms in the United States and a number of larger players that primarily have a strong presence abroad.

ANSWERTHINK

www.answerthink.com

Founded in 1997 by former KPMG partners, business and technology consultancy Answerthink offers process benchmarking, business transformation, business application services, and technology integration. It also owns The Hackett Group, a business process advisory firm, drawing on its best-practice research for engagements. Answerthink has seven offices in the U.S., Europe, and Asia.

AVENUE A | RAZORFISH

www.avenuea-razorfish.com

SBI.Razorfish was acquired by aQuantive in 2004, then combined with Avenue A, the largest independent buyer of online media and search. Razorfish's services include interactive marketing, customer-focused websites, e-commerce, intranets/extranets, and branding and identity. Clients include Coors Brewing Company, Carnival Cruise Lines, Nielsen Media, and Ford.

CAMBRIDGE ASSOCIATES LLC

www.cambridgeassociates.com

Cambridge Associates provides investment and financial research, consulting, and advisory services, and represents three-quarters of U.S. higher education endowment assets. It has offices in Boston; Dallas; Arlington, Virginia; Menlo Park, California; London; and Singapore.

CIBER INC.

www.ciber.com

Ciber, a system integrator with more than 8,000 employees and $956 million in 2005 revenue, added SCB Computer Technology, Ascent Technology, and the services arm of FullTilt in 2004 and Knowledge Systems, an India-based professional services firm, in 2005. Its clients include General Motors, the Commonwealth of Pennsylvania, U.S. Postal Service, IBM, Cornell University, DaimlerChrysler, and the state of Texas. Based in Greenwood Village, Colorado, Ciber has offices in 18 countries.

FMI CORPORATION

www.fminet.com

FMI serves the construction and design industry with strategy development and implementation and investment banking. The firm has offices in Denver, Tampa, and Raleigh, North Carolina, and employs more than 150 professionals.

HP SERVICES

www.hp.com/hps

HP may be best known for printers, computers, servers, and networking hardware, but services made the company around $15.5 billion in 2005—a healthy 12 percent gain over 2004—and includes 69,000 professionals. HP competes with other technology consulting firms such as IBM and EDS to design, build, integrate, and manage IT infrastructure.

HURON CONSULTING GROUP

www.huronconsultinggroup.com

Founded in 2002 by some 213 former Andersen consultants, Huron has grown quickly. Today, it has more than 770 employees and in 2005 saw revenue rise nearly 30 percent to $207 million. The firm offers financial and operational consulting services to help clients deal with issues such as litigation, disputes, investigations, and regulation. In 2006, it acquired Galt & Company, a firm that designs and implements programs to improve shareholder returns, adding close to 30 consultants.

KEANE, INC.

www.keane.com

Keane is a 9,500-person, $955 million IT services firm serving the Global 2000. Founded in 1965, Keane offers business process outsourcing and application services. It is pursuing a global operating model. Headquartered in Boston, the firm has offices across North America, the United Kingdom, India, and Australia.

KURT SALMON ASSOCIATES INC.

www.kurtsalmon.com

Kurt Salmon Associates, founded in 1935 by a German textile engineer (and the company's namesake), provides strategy, process, and technology deployment solutions to the consumer products/retail and health care industries. Teams consist of two to ten consultants and are informal and highly participatory, and generally work onsite. Headquartered in Atlanta, Kurt Salmon has seven offices in the United States and Mexico, six in Europe, and five in Asia.

LOGICACMG CONSULTING

www.logicacmg.com

LogicaCMG Consulting is the management consulting arm of LogicaCMG, a large European-headquartered systems integrator. It provides management and IT consulting, systems development and integration, and outsourcing. LogicaCMG was formed in December 2002 when Logica merged with CMG. The firm employs 30,000 people across 36 countries.

MARKETBRIDGE CORP.

www.market-bridge.com

Founded as Oxford Associates in 1991 and headquartered in Bethesda, Maryland, Marketbridge consults on sales processes. It helps organizations design, build, integrate, and manage multichannel sales applications, targeting the Fortune 500. Its CEO, Tim Furey, is coauthor of *The Channel Advantage*. The firm has five offices in North America and Europe.

MERCER INC.

www.mercer.com

Mercer, parent company of Mercer Management Consulting—profiled in the "Major Players" section—also offers HR, investment, organizational, economic, and identity and brand strategy consulting services. Mercer, which is owned by public firm Marsh & McLennan Companies (ticker: MMC), had $3.8 billion in revenue in 2005, and more than 16,000 employees.

MILLIMAN, INC.

www.milliman.com

Milliman combines actuarial and business experience to provide consulting services on employee benefits, health care, life insurance and financial services, and property and casualty services. Founded in 1947, the firm has 850 consultants and actuaries in 31 U.S. offices, and belongs to Milliman Global. Revenue in 2005 was $435 million; Milliman Global's was $579 million.

RIGHT MANAGEMENT CONSULTANTS

www.right.com

Founded in 1980, Right Management Consultants provides career transition and organizational consulting. After an acquisition blitz—Right bought Coutts Consulting in 2002 after making eight acquisitions in 2001 and four in 2000—Manpower acquired the firm in 2003. Right operates as a wholly owned subsidiary and earned $24.5 million for Manpower in 2005, the same as in 2004.

SAPIENT CORPORATION

www.sapient.com

Sapient, which was founded in 1991, ran into problems after the Internet bubble burst, but has since made a resurgence, as evidenced by strong revenue growth and its placement on *Consulting Magazine*'s 2005 list of the "Ten Best Consulting Firms to Work For". It works with its clients to plan, create, and manage business-critical technology-based solutions—from e-business and Web strategy to supply chain services, application management, and outsourcing. The firm, which has more than 3,000 employees, saw revenue rise 20 percent in 2005 to $333 million. In 2006, it acquired Planning Group International, an integrated marketing agency specializing in online, offline, and multi-channel marketing strategies. Sapient made *Consulting Magazine*'s list of "Ten Best Firms to Work For" in 2005.

SDG CORPORATION

www.sdg.com

SDG (which stands for Strategic Decisions Group, its original name) was acquired by Navigant in 1999 and separated just 19 months later in a management buyout. The firm's roughly 150 employees work primarily with Fortune 500 companies to increase shareholder value. SDG consults on issues such as realignment and prioritization of businesses, optimizing investments, divestiture, and applying new technologies. Check out the firm's 2003 book, *Solving the Corporate Value Enigma: A System to Unlock Shareholder Value*, to find out more about the firm's thinking.

TOWERS PERRIN

www.towersperrin.com

Towers Perrin includes Tillinghast for insurance industry and risk management consulting, Towers Perrin Reinsurance for reinsurance consulting, and HR Services. The firm was founded in 1934 under the name Towers, Perrin, Foster & Crosby and started out specializing in reinsurance, pension, and employee benefits. The company changed its name to Towers Perrin in 1987. It has offices in 25 countries.

UNISYS CORPORATION

www.unisys.com

Unisys, a 132-year-old company with origins in the typewriter business, took its current name when Sperry and Burroughs merged in 1986. It may be better known for its mainframe computers than for its consulting services, but like HP and IBM Global Services, it offers systems integration, outsourcing, infrastructure, and server technology services.

ZS ASSOCIATES

www.zsassociates.com

Established in 1983 by two professors from Northwestern, ZS Associates focuses on sales and marketing management consulting. The firm has seven North American offices, four in Europe, one in Tokyo, and one in Pune, India, and employs 600 professionals.

On the Job

What Exactly Does a Consultant Do?

Associate

Consultant

Senior Consultant

Senior Manager

What Exactly Does a Consultant Do?

Consultants are hired advisers to business—usually big business. In this role they tackle a variety of issues, all of which ultimately boil down to a few central themes. Consultants define problems, develop methodologies for solving problems, collect data that will help solve problems, and—you guessed it—solve problems. Although the precise focus of the work varies from firm to firm, consultants tend to work on issues that will have a major impact on a client's organization, such as how to streamline manufacturing processes to save money, open a new distribution channel over the Web, or reorganize divisions to save money and increase productivity. More often than not, consultants work in teams that report directly to the client's CEO or other top management.

TYPICAL PROJECTS

The standard consulting fare is similar across firms. A given firm might specialize in a particular type of project, such as reengineering or systems work, but based on our interviews with many people at different firms, the following sample projects are fairly representative of what you're likely to encounter. Remember, the actual work you do will depend on the approach and strategy of your firm, and possibly the unit you join.

Operations and Strategy

A large high-tech company asks a consulting firm to help it determine the best location for a new plant. The consultant examines the qualitative and quantitative costs and benefits of locating in different countries, regions, cities, or towns, makes recommendations to the client's management team, and negotiates on the client's behalf to acquire a particular site.

Acquisition Study

A medical device manufacturer sees an opportunity to increase its value by expanding its product line. It hires a consulting firm to help it confidentially evaluate several targets for acquisition and determine a fair market price. After extensive market research and a thorough valuation of the opportunity, the client authorizes the consulting firm to approach management of the target company and initiate discussions about a potential acquisition.

E-Commerce Study

A large consumer products company wants to step up its Web presence to better market toiletries to consumers. It engages a strategy-consulting firm to probe its target audience to find out its habits, concerns, and desires related to the Internet and personal-care products. The project team interviews people and observes them browsing the Internet, noting which sites they visit, how they use the sites, what types of functionality appeal to them, and other issues related to their online behavior. In addition, it draws up questions for a series of focus groups that are run by an outside market research firm. The team takes all this data and makes a case for how the client should use the Internet for its personal-care business—arguing, for instance, that the client use the Web for brand-building. The team then makes recommendations on how to do that, such as creating a portal dedicated to household and personal hygiene issues where people can get quick, seemingly objective advice for running a more comfortable and efficient household.

Operations and Strategy, Redux

A regional bank wants to become more competitive in the home mortgage market. It hires a consulting firm to analyze the competition, identify other banks' best practices, and conduct a review of the bank's own operations. Based on its findings, the consultant recommends and subsequently works with bank staff to implement changes to the review process for loan applications. It then installs new systems for evaluating and tracking the loan portfolio and trains employees in their use.

PROJECT CYCLE

A typical project (or engagement) for a consulting firm can last from a month to several years. During that time, the work usually goes through several phases. Depending on the type of study, a typical project starts with defining the problem and its expected outcomes and developing a work plan for the project. It continues with each team member collecting the information necessary to analyze a particular question. Finally, the team draws on the information collected and provides recommendations for action. Increasingly, consultants are also getting involved in nuts-and-bolts implementation work, which may be done either as a follow-up project or as part of the original project. In other words, they roll up their sleeves and do the actual work they recommended to the client.

TEAM STRUCTURE

A consulting project is generally handled by a team, which can vary in size from two people (or in some cases, one consultant plus members from the client organization) to hundreds. The size of a project team will depend on the nature of the work and the philosophy of the firm. Many strategy-oriented firms staff teams with five or six people from different levels. In contrast, IT projects may have dozens of people developing and implementing a new software system. As you might imagine, the bulk of the programming and design work for such projects is handled by junior employees, who bill out at lower rates. You may be able to get a feel for how a firm staffs its projects by comparing its revenue with the number of professionals—a high revenue per consultant generally indicates a high percentage of senior-level staff.

CLIENT INTERACTIONS

A critical part of any consultant's work is his or her interactions with the client. More and more these days, consulting firms are attempting to integrate client staff into project teams, though different firms have different ways of doing so. Many firms rely on client staff to be key resources, while others use client staff as active participants in project definition and research. Particularly in the case of reengineering projects, the consultant often trains client staff members in new ways of thinking about their business.

KEY JOBS

As each firm has its favorite buzzwords, it also has unique terminology for its rank and file. While the titles might vary from firm to firm, the roles can basically be divided as follows: analyst (also called research associate or staff consultant at some firms), consultant (or senior consultant), manager, and partner or VP. In addition, consulting firms hire a cadre of highly capable nonprofessional staff into administrative and support positions. (This is not a bad place to be if you've got skills in PowerPoint and you like to create slides.)

Administrative Assistant

Most consulting firms have a fairly large pool of college-educated administrative assistants and support staff on board so that the consultants can keep focused on tasks that justify their $200-plus per hour billing rates. In addition to performing standard support functions, many have specific roles (recruiting, office administration, or website maintenance, for example). Most firms also have a group of graphic designers on staff to prepare materials for presentations.

Salary range: $30,000 to $50,000 or more

Analyst/Research Associate/Staff Consultant

This is the position at the bottom of the professional pyramid. The vast bulk of analysts are young, talented, and hungry college graduates. Many firms structure this position to last for two to three years, after which the analyst is expected to move on—perhaps to graduate school or another employer. (Some firms do allow people to progress up the management ladder without leaving the firm.) The work itself—as well as the hours—can be quite demanding. It often includes field research, data analysis, customer and competitor interviews, and client meetings. In IT, analysts might do heavy-duty programming.

Salary range: $35,000 to $75,000, plus a signing bonus or year-end bonus

Associate/Consultant/Senior Consultant

This is the typical port of entry for newly minted MBAs (and increasingly for other graduate students as well). Senior consultants often perform research and analysis, formulate recommendations, and present findings to the client. Oh, and at many firms, they have to implement those great ideas, too. Although this is usually a tenure-track position, a fair number of consultants will leave the business after two or three years to pursue entrepreneurial or industry positions.

Salary range: $70,000 to $130,000 or more, with bonus

Manager

After a few years, a senior consultant will move up to manager. As the title implies, this usually means leading a team of consultants and analysts toward project completion. Some firms may hire MBAs with significant work experience directly into the manager position, particularly in their IT practices. In addition to having more rigorous responsibilities for managing the project team, the manager will typically be a primary point person for client interactions.

Salary range: $75,000 to $150,000

Partner or VP

Congratulations! You've forded the River Jordan of consulting and arrived at the Promised Land. Note that some firms further subdivide partners into junior and senior grades. And, if you aspire to it, there's always chairman or CEO. As a partner, one of your big responsibilities will be to bring in new work. Fortunately, as with other big-ticket sales jobs, the pay can be quite rewarding.

Salary range: $250,000 to several million dollars at leading firms

A WEEK IN THE LIFE OF A CONSULTANT

Monday

Beginning at 8 a.m., I start looking at articles on one of my firm's high-tech client's competitors. Spend a few hours reading and documenting the articles. Around 10:30 a.m., spend some time on the phone setting up interviews with our client's customers. I also develop an interview guide to use when I talk to them. The articles help me come up with specific questions for this guide. In particular, I'm interested in the level of service our client provides. In the afternoon, get together with other team members to discuss what we want to learn from the interviews—they have some ideas that will be useful for my guide. Leave the office around 6 p.m.

Tuesday

Take a 7 a.m. flight to Atlanta, where I conduct the interviews I set up the day before. As I talk to different customers, I adjust my questions. As the conversations go on, it becomes increasingly clear that unlike its competitors, the client is not providing a key aspect of service to its customers. Get to my hotel around 6 p.m., order room service, and eat a hamburger while slouched over my laptop, typing up interview notes. I then try to summarize on one page the most important things I learned. Finish around 9:30 p.m.

Wednesday

Spend the day at the client's office in a suburb of Atlanta. In the morning, meet with members of the client team to discuss where we are in our analysis and to come up with a presentation. We talk about what I learned from customers, and the client team shares some of the modeling they've done on their internal numbers. We involve my manager by conference call as we discuss the implications of this information and the recommendations we plan to make at the Thursday presentation. Then we work on the content of the presentation: We're going to give it to the client leader tomorrow. Our graphics department does the typing and graphs, and the client team edits them. Around 8 p.m., I have dinner with my manager, another consultant on the team, and a client team member.

Thursday

In the morning, we deliver the presentation to a senior manager at the client organization. I present some of the work, the client team members present some, and my manager presents some. The client senior manager is not surprised at what I learned, but asks a lot of follow-up questions about what she should do about it. I'm not ready to answer these questions. We discuss her ideas and then decide to conduct several more interviews before making any decisions. I catch a 6:30 p.m. flight back to Boston with my manager, but we don't get in until 10:45 p.m., because the flight is delayed by thunderstorms.

Friday

Back at the office. Spend the morning in internal meetings about recruiting and training. I also meet with my team to discuss the next steps for the project I've been working on all week. Cut out of the office around 4 p.m.—after all, it's Friday.

Associate

Age: 25
Years in business: three
Education: BS in economics, Vanderbilt University
Size of company: 1,500 employees
Hours per week: 50, 8 a.m. to 6 p.m.; an hour for lunch, but that varies depending on the project.
Annual salary: $55,000, plus bonus

How did you get your job?

I was recruited on my college campus. As is the case with most management consulting firms, this was a highly competitive selection process.

What are your career aspirations?

I definitely want to stay in the business world. I'll probably remain with this firm for a couple more years. After that, I'll consider either staying in consulting or moving into a management position somewhere else in the business world. And at some point, of course, I'll get my MBA.

What kinds of people do well in this business?

You have to be really interested in business. This is not an academic group or a non-profit, though occasionally we have clients in those areas. Our focus is on large business corporations. You also have to be a team player. If you prefer to work by yourself, this is the wrong job for you. Finally, you must have exceptional analytical skills, and not just in an academic way. In this profession, you need to be able to figure out what your suggestions will mean for the client, which may require a more intuitive analysis.

What do you really like about your job?

I like the fact that I can have a significant impact on a large organization, even at a relatively young age. I also enjoy the challenges posed by the problems themselves—the sheer variety of issues we have to deal with is interesting. And management consulting firms tend to hire top-notch individuals. It's exciting to work with so many bright people.

What do you dislike?

I travel anywhere from zero to three days a week, sometimes more. After a while, it can be extremely draining.

What is the biggest misconception about this job?

Three things come to mind, actually. First is the myth that consultants do everything in a vacuum. We work intensely with our clients in developing recommendations; we don't just sit around in our offices writing up a report that will land on the client's desk when we're through. The second myth is that we don't stick around to see our suggestions implemented. We do provide our clients assistance through the implementation phase. The third misconception is that it's impossible to have an impact as a junior employee. If you can make a compelling and meaningful analysis of a situation, you can have a substantial impact on the outcome of a case. Personally, I have even had the opportunity to manage a client team of 20 people working on the implementation of the recommendations that were made by our team. I don't sit in my office doing spreadsheets all day.

How can someone get a job like yours?

Logistically speaking, the most common way, for an undergraduate at least, is through on-campus recruiting. Prospective applicants can also contact the recruiting department of a firm directly, if they're not on a campus where there is active recruiting. Once you've got the interview, the things that will actually get you hired are your analytical skills, communication skills, and presence. Demonstrated leadership potential is another quality they look for, so if you've held leadership positions in the past, it will be to your advantage—but you want to show them that you did more than just hold an office. Show your interviewer that you excelled at whatever you were doing. There is no cookie-cutter mold for a management consultant. There are lots of ways to demonstrate that you are a person with drive and potential.

Describe a typical day.

7:00 a.m. Get to the office. I'm working on a project for a retail client, a children's clothing company. Status check on my team's deliverable, in this case a presentation to the client's board of directors. Quiet time. What needs to be done to finish the presentation? I do this every day to plan my day.

7:30 a.m. Try to chase down people on the client team to get some answers to questions I've come up with. Hope they get back to me by the end of the day. Want to find out what they're planning in terms of color coordinates for the next season. I let them know what I've learned about what competitors might be doing.

8:00 a.m. Personal email time. My friends outside the company know that this is the best time to call me to chat.

9:00 a.m. Back to work. Review market data. This means crunching through our database of customer survey responses. We go beyond just reporting what the client's best customers are like demographically. Find out what their shopping habits are. We also look for even more detailed information—for example, whether they are more concerned with price or quality, and whether they want a range of clothing for all ages of children or just for the under-age-seven crowd that is already the client's main focus.

12:00 p.m. Lunch with friends.

1:00 p.m. Attend a case team meeting. The case is modular—meaning that we all work on different pieces—so we need to share information. One woman is working on pricing, and I'm working on trends, so I tell her about an article that says that discount children's clothing is becoming more popular.

2:30 p.m. Before ending the meeting, we make sure via a conference call that people outside the office know what's going on.

3:00 p.m.   More email.

3:20 p.m.   Look at masses of marketing material and articles to figure out trends. Should the client focus more on babies? If you want the client to narrow its customer base and still make more money, you have to do your research to show how this will happen. Spend some time doing research: current and projected birthrate in the United States, average amount people spend on their own children's clothing versus those of friends and relatives, and potential competition from retailers ranging from discount stores to neighborhood boutiques.

6:00 p.m.   Calls from clients start to come in. Spend about half an hour talking with each person.

8:00 p.m.   Go home.

Consultant

Age: 29
Education: MBA
Size of company: More than 10,000 people
Hours per week: 40 to 60
Annual salary: $85,000 to $110,000

How did you get your job?

Campus recruiting. I spent a lot of time with cases—the interviews were very case-heavy. I'd recommend having a clear sense about the different firms. What's interesting about specific firms? Keep an open mind, too. Find out as much as you can about the culture of the firms. You could end up at a high prestige firm and be miserable, because you're working with people you don't enjoy being with.

What are your career aspirations?

They're not really typical for a consultant. I want to get into nonprofit management. I'm interested in working for a foundation or an organization that's promoting social change. I'd like to apply the strategy stuff I'm learning to the nonprofit world, or do something in corporate social responsibility.

What kinds of people do well in this business?

You have to be very flexible, that's the first thing. My project is ending in Friday, and I have no idea where I'll be working two weeks from now. When I talked to staffing, there was a possibility I'd be in California, a possibility I'd be in Minneapolis, and a possibility neither would work out and I'd be in Podunk, Idaho. You have to really be people-oriented, and understand what it's like to work with people at a very high level in organizations and get things done.

What do you really like about your job?

I like the challenge of it. It's fun to be doing different things all the time. You're working with high-level people who are really sharp. It can be stressful, but it can be a lot of fun. I've had nothing but good experiences with the people I work with. This is sometimes a stressful job, so it's important you work with good people, or it can be pretty hard.

What do you dislike?

The travel—being gone four days a week is tiring. That's the number one thing. It can be stressful. If you get on a project that's really demanding, it can mean a lot of hours.

What is the biggest misconception about this job?

People who go into this job see it as a glamorous profession. It is to a certain extent. You are helping to shape strategy for companies. But there's a lot of grunt work, too. You won't spend all your time schmoozing with CEOs, especially in your first year. Like any job, it has its pros and cons.

How can someone get a job like yours?

My firm recruits on a lot of campuses, so that's a good place to start if you're a student. You have to demonstrate an interest in consulting. It's something you have to want to do, and have good reasons for wanting to do it. You have to prove to the people you're talking to that you'll make a good consultant. They have a big pool to choose from. We work with a lot of large companies, so having corporate experience can be helpful—knowing how big companies work. You have to demonstrate that you're smart and flexible, and can look at a problem and break it down.

Describe a typical day.

It depends on the project. We're working on a strategy project right now, analyzing a study we did for a client. The work depends on the stage of the project. I spent some time on calls talking to high-level people, trying to figure out what's going on in the industry and what's important to the companies they're working with. Right now, I'm putting together a series of presentations for different CEOs. Taking ideas and putting them in a form that's clear, precise, and logical that people can connect with. My last project was entirely different; I was working on a client site doing change management.

Senior Consultant

Age: 27
Years in business: two
Education: BS in finance and marketing, Duke University; MBA, Harvard University
Hours per week: 55 to 75; at the worst, 7 a.m. to 10 p.m., depending on travel
Size of company: 100 employees
Annual salary: $110,000, plus bonus

How did you get your job?

I got my job through on-campus recruiting. I knew from a previous internship at a large management consulting firm that I wanted to work for a smaller company. So I did research on about 20 different firms, then interviewed at about ten of them that came to our campus. I worked my way up to senior consultant, a step below the case manager on a case team. It's my job to help define the objectives of our analyses and the deliverables. I do a lot of coordinating and communicating with both the clients and the rest of the team, and I delegate responsibilities to analysts and less senior consultants.

What are your career aspirations?

I got into consulting because I wanted to stay on a fast-paced learning curve after I finished business school. Someday I hope to use what I have learned to start my own business, perhaps in low-tech manufacturing or in software or Internet services.

What kinds of people do well in this business?

You must have strong analytical skills. Quantitative skills are an especially big asset, as there is less of a need in consulting for purely qualitative analysis. You must like to learn and to work hard and be able to think fast. Above all, though, you need interpersonal skills—especially with clients—because in the end, this is a sales job. You have to be able to sell your ideas to clients, or all of the work that you did in formulating the ideas means nothing.

What do you really like about your job?

I like the challenge of solving a complex problem for people who have not been able to solve it for themselves. There is a lot of adrenaline—and stress—involved when you begin facing a problem that you don't necessarily know how to solve at the outset. Then, when you find the answer, it's extremely satisfying. I also enjoy the customer interaction a lot. Another thing I like about my firm specifically is that, because it's small, I was able to take on authority and responsibility more quickly than I could have at a larger firm.

What do you dislike?

The traveling gets old. My wife thinks so, too.

What is the biggest misconception about this job?

Many people think it's more glamorous than it is. When you're a young guy who shows up at a client firm as a consultant, wearing an expensive suit, people are either going to think, "What a stud," or "This jerk thinks he knows everything." Neither of these perceptions is really fair. When you get right down to it, consulting involves hard work and personal inconvenience. Despite what you may know about the established knowledge management principles that exist at some firms, most of the time these principles aren't effective when applied to an actual case. The individual consultants have to put in a lot of hours, do a lot of research, and spend a lot of time in a place they'd rather not be to come up with a proposal that will work—which isn't very glamorous.

How can someone get a job like yours?

Go to Harvard Business School. No, seriously, just get an MBA. That's the best way—the firms will come looking for you. Even if you don't have an MBA or any desire to obtain one, you can still get a job in consulting by going after the firms yourself. Consulting firms are hiring higher percentages of PhDs and JDs than ever before. Anyone who has had good academic results and who prepares well for the case interviews should stand a good chance of landing a job.

Describe a typical day.

8:00 a.m. First thing in the morning, at home, check my email and voice mail. After I hear my messages, I begin to plan my day.

9:00 a.m. Arrive at the office and begin to focus on producing deliverables for various clients. I often spend 10 to 12 hours a day working on these.

10:30 a.m. The case team meets to discuss progress and objectives for our most important project.

12:00 p.m. I never spend more than a half-hour having lunch. Today I have Chinese takeout.

12:30 p.m. Back in my office, working on a deliverable. In this case, it's a fairly in-depth marketing analysis. Frequently, I'm interrupted by phone calls. Send email and voicemail to clients and case managers, answering their questions.

4:00 p.m. Talk with a client on the phone to do some preliminary data-gathering before my trip to his site next week. When I'm through with this, I get back to work on the deliverables I've been working on since the morning.

6:00 p.m. Calling it quits for today, but before I leave, spend some time thinking about deadlines and project goals. Send a few more emails out to some analysts on the team, delegating some number-crunching tasks to them.

Senior Manager

Age: 45
Years in business: five
Education: MBA
Hours per week: 50, plus 8 hours of travel
Annual salary: $125,000, plus bonus

What do you do?

I'm a project manager. I make sure that we deliver on the promises we made when the services were sold. I manage a group of people to get a system running or otherwise achieve a business benefit like reducing inventory, improving customer service, or shrinking the time it takes to figure out what a factory should be making.

How did you get your job?

Networking. I knew a retired partner of the firm and asked for a referral. He put me in touch with a partner and I emailed my resume. It went through the recruiting team, and a hiring manager called me. What you have to understand is that in a huge organization there are many tiny businesses inside the organization, and you work on virtual teams. I interviewed with the people in the city where I'd be working, went to California for another interview, and had a phone interview with a guy in Boston. It's not common to be hired in at the level of senior manager, so it requires approval at a certain level. The funny thing is that I realized the day before my phone interview that I used to work with the guy in Boston. When you've been in a field for 5, 10, or 15 years, it's not the same as when you're just getting out of college.

What are your career aspirations?

Partner. You have your own little business you run with a profit and loss statement. The difference between partner and senior manager is that as partner you have to worry about making money. You have to make sure your business holds together financially.

> **All firms are different, and the products are different. If someone tells me they're going to work as a consultant, that really doesn't tell me anything at all.**

What kind of person does really well at this job?

Someone who has good people skills, listens and communicates well, and can do the normal supervisory stuff like letting people know when they're doing a good job. You have to listen to what the clients are explaining. In general, consulting requires someone who values information and stimulation, someone who enjoys being on the leading edge of a new concept. It's information overload. You have to be able to sift through to the important stuff. It also takes a lot of self-confidence.

What do you really like about your job?

There are always more things to know and learn. You're solving important business problems. The key difference between consulting and industry is that in industry you only get really important problems to solve every couple of years, maybe only several times in your career. In consulting, every problem is important.

What do you dislike?

You lose control of your time. Your client or boss can call and tell you to be in a different city tomorrow. It's very hard to plan the kind of vacation where you reserve a condo six months ahead. Every weekend, you have a long list of things to do, and you never get enough time to do them.

What is the biggest misconception about this job?

To consider all consulting the same way. All firms are different, and the products are different. If someone tells me they're going to work as a consultant, that really doesn't tell me anything at all. When I first got into the field, I was asked what kind of consulting I wanted to do, and I had no idea. I didn't know how important that question was. That's the most important question: What kind of consulting do you want to do?

How does someone get a job like yours?

Contact people who work in consulting. You can go to career fairs and look on the Internet for where to send your resume. But the best way is to identify where you want to work, and find someone who works there. You don't have to know them. It can be a friend of a friend.

Describe a typical day.

7:00 a.m. Arrive at my cubicle at the client's office and check email and voicemail. In terms of infrastructure, I have the same setup as the client's employees: a cubicle, email, and voicemail. I may be here six to nine months, so I have two sets of email and voicemail to check—here and at my office at the consulting firm.

8:00 a.m. Look at my calendar and plan my day. Today, I decide to postpone a group meeting on one topic, so we can work on a presentation we're making. Our client is a large corporation made up of many different groups. We were hired by one particular group, but there's very little they can achieve as just one group acting alone. We help them recruit allies from other groups in the company. Our presentation is designed to help them gain larger visibility in the company. The presentation is divided into different sections. I work alone on my part, which is to identify industry best practices. I look at an internal database and find three different resources that have relevant information, and put that into a couple of PowerPoint slides.

12:00 p.m.   Go to the company cafeteria for lunch and then take a walk outside because it's a nice day.

1:00 p.m.   Return to work on the presentation.

3:00 p.m.   Meet with the project team. Consulting company members are seated on the project team with client company members. Each of us presents our piece. We decide what holes we have to work on and where changes are needed.

4:00 p.m.   Make the changes necessary in my part.

5:00 p.m.   Meet with my consulting firm boss. He's also located on site at the client's office. We discuss whether we're doing all the right things to meet the client's expectations. A team member is leaving to join the competition, and we discuss how to best replace him. You do the same networking thing as when you look for a job: You tell everybody you know that you're looking for someone. First we look internally, then for subcontractors. Getting a new hire from outside probably won't happen fast enough.

6:00 p.m.   Go to dinner. Sometimes it's business, but tonight I'm alone. Afterward, I check my email and voicemail again. The email has information about new business wins, training that's available, and requests for people to work on projects. I get requests from firm members all over the world asking questions in my area of expertise, and I want to tell them what I know. In a firm of this size, you have a lot of resources at your disposal. If I need to talk to somebody in Australia, there isn't very much of a window when we'll both be awake. With email, I can answer a request before I go to sleep, and he'll have the information he needs when he gets up. It keeps things moving faster.

The Workplace

Lifestyle

Hours and Travel

Diversity

Vacation

Compensation

Career Path

Insider Scoop

Lifestyle

The consulting lifestyle is known for being arduous. It is also relatively fast-paced, with consultants jetting around the country to client sites and working from deadline to deadline to gather lots of data to provide a client with a solid recommendation for action. As a consultant, you can expect to eat out a lot, almost never get home early, and rack up plenty of frequent flyer miles. Major partying (and doing laundry, paying bills, shopping, and socializing) will usually have to wait until the weekend. Beware: It can be a difficult way to live. "I do not find it to be a sustainable lifestyle," says one insider. "There are people who I'm sure can sustain it, but, all in all, it's hard. It's the hours, but even more than that, it's the intensity; it's the travel. Even when you aren't at work, you still know you could be getting that voicemail at night."

When choosing a firm, make sure you like the people. The demands of the consulting lifestyle are such that unless you get along well with the people you're working with, they can be hard to take. One of the reasons why firms put so much stress on "fit" is because when you work long hours, often under the pressure of deadlines, collegial relationships (and working with team players) can make or break a case—and a consultant.

Hours and Travel

On average, most consultants work 55 to 60 hours in a typical week. However, as everyone you speak to will tell you, there is no typical week. Before a presentation or a deadline, you may need to put in 80, 90, or even 100 hours, possibly including an all-nighter or two. In contrast, the time between projects, or during liberally staffed projects, may be relatively slow. Even so, consulting is not a nine-to-five job. Hours vary by firm, by office, and by practice, so you'll want to ask about hours before accepting an offer.

Consultants travel often and for days at a time. Although firms vary in their emphasis on the need to be at the client site, the primary factors affecting the amount of travel are the location of the client and the type of project. On average, a new undergrad or MBA hire can expect to be on the road at least two days a week. During a project, however, it is not uncommon to spend four days at the client site, week after week.

Diversity

Consulting firms tend to look a lot like the Ivy League schools where they recruit. There's not a lot of diversity, though like the brochures of those Ivy League schools, the recruiting material tells a different story. Nevertheless, firms are trying to diversify their ranks. When you apply to a firm, you might want to ask about its diversity recruiting efforts and its success in retaining minority talent. Some minority and female professionals may be discouraged by the dearth of minorities and women in the manager-level ranks and above. Make sure you're comfortable at the firm and that there's room for you to rise; it's worth inquiring about minorities and women in management positions, introducing yourself to them, and discussing your career goals and how supportive the firm will be as you move toward those goals.

Vacation

Most firms offer new employees about three weeks of vacation per year, though it might be hard to take much of that time off mid-project. Project breaks provide a good opportunity to get away, and one big perk is that you'll have enough frequent flier miles to travel almost anywhere in the world (provided you want to get on a plane again). Also, even if you don't take a formal vacation, most firms discourage a nine-to-five mentality. As a result, insiders report that you can often take a day or two off after a particularly grueling period.

Compensation

The major consulting firms are among the best-paying employers for new graduates, though the gap between consulting and industry has narrowed somewhat over the last few years, as industry has been catching up. Consulting firms are also known for offering excellent perks and benefits, such as annual offsite meetings at posh resorts and reimbursement of school expenses. At strategy firms, salaries notched up slightly in both 2005 and 2006. Billing rates have generally stagnated, and many firms have been moving a larger portion of pay into variable compensation programs, which become a bigger factor the longer you're at a firm.

Salaries and bonus packages at the top firms are generally in close range of each other, since these firms usually compete for the same pool of candidates. At the margins, there are slight differences in compensation: Lesser-known firms may offer slightly higher salaries or bonuses to attract top candidates, and some organizations have different ways of splitting up the bonus pie (for instance, linking a portion of the bonus to the firm's annual performance). To get more specific information on compensation practices, check out WetFeet's individual company Insider Guides, available at www.wetfeet.com.

SPECIAL INFORMATION FOR UNDERGRADUATES

Competition for hiring college graduates has been strong in 2006, leading to higher salaries, according to the National Association of Colleges and Employers—good news for prospective consultants. In the 2006–07 recruiting season, we estimate that the elite firms will offer starting salaries in the range of $50,000 to $70,000, with signing bonuses of up to $10,000. Undergraduates joining a large IT services firm will likely be in the $40,000 to $60,000 range to start.

SPECIAL INFORMATION FOR MBAS

In 2006–07, we estimate that MBAs hired into elite firms will start with an average base salary in the range of $110,000 to $125,000, with signing bonuses between 5 and 20 percent of the base, and performance bonuses between 5 and 30 percent. Total compensation is expected to be in the $120,000 to $135,000 range.

In 2006, *Consultants News* reported an average base salary for MBAs of $111,000, and an average signing bonus of $14,000, both up 2 percent over 2005. Signing bonuses ranged from $10,000 to $17,000, and base pay between $109,000 and $115,000.

Although consultants often have higher base salaries than investment bankers, bankers stand to make lots more—as much as 100 percent of their base—from their year-end bonuses. That's why some junior partners on Wall Street make more money than senior partners at consulting firms.

Career Path

UNDERGRADUATES

Undergraduates generally join a consulting firm as analysts, although their titles vary. Traditionally, the analyst program lasts two to three years, after which you're encouraged to go to business school. However, this system has been changing over the past several years. Firms have increasingly begun to promote analysts into positions previously reserved for MBAs or into interim roles between the undergraduate and MBA position. If you choose to go to business school, many firms will pay your tuition, provided you return to the firm when you're done.

MBAS

Consulting firms hire MBAs and other postgraduates right out of school or from industry. Most new MBA hires will come into a firm as associates; after two or three years they'll move to the next level, where they'll manage case teams. After managing projects for a couple of years, consultants may be promoted to principal, whereupon the focus shifts to more intensive client work and the selling of services. Finally, after seven to ten years with a firm, a consultant might be promoted to partner. The benefits of partnership include big increases in salary and responsibility. The key function of partners at most firms is to cultivate clients and sell them the firm's services.

ADVANCED-DEGREE CANDIDATES

Consulting firms often tap nontraditional candidate pools, including JDs, PhDs, and MDs. If you are one of these candidates, find out which level you'll come in at: either the same level as undergrads, MBAs, or experienced hires. Also, you should ask about the type of support you'll receive once you join the firm. Some organizations offer a mini-MBA training program, while others rely more heavily on mentorship.

Insider Scoop

WHAT EMPLOYEES REALLY LIKE

Love My Job

Consultants generally find a high degree of satisfaction in the intellectual stimulation they get from their work. "The work is just phenomenal," one insider says. They enjoy the challenge of going into new settings and facing some of the most difficult issues business leaders have to deal with. Although most don't admit it openly, there's also a palpable excitement associated with being able to sit down with a CEO of a large firm and tell that CEO what they ought to do. Consultants also take pride in seeing the impact their advice has on clients' businesses.

People Power

The key resource of consulting firms, and some would say the only resource, is their people. All of the top-tier firms fill their offices by skimming the cream of the undergraduate and business school elite. Insiders tell us that working at a consulting firm feels very much like being on a team with the best people from school: "People are universally bright, interesting, hardworking, and motivated." (Sounds a little self-congratulatory, but it seems to be true.) Many insiders also say they enjoy socializing with their colleagues. A common refrain is, "These are people I'd be hanging out with anyway, even if we didn't work together."

Learning Environment

One of the thrills for many consultants is the constant learning that comes with the consulting workload. Whether you're learning about a new company or industry, talking to people in various divisions of a client organization, or brainstorming ways to deal with challenging technical problems, consulting offers a steady diet of new cases and settings. Many consultants believe they wouldn't face such a wide variety of challenges in another profession.

Pay and Perks

Very few consultants would publicly put it at the top of their lists, but most really like the pay and perks of the position. Even if you're not a particularly money-grubbing type, wouldn't you like to be able to afford a nice apartment, a new car, and to be able to pay off all those school loans in a couple of years? Moreover, many firms provide reimbursement of tuition expenses for some of their employees. Beyond that, all of the firms make sure that the extensive travel and the long hours are as manageable as possible. Even if you don't relish the idea of staying in Phoenix for the next three months, you probably won't mind staying at the Phoenician Hotel.

Future Options

Many people enter consulting with the idea that they'll do it for a couple of years and then move on to something else. "It's hands-down the best job for someone [planning to start] a business or work at a Fortune 500 company. You can get behind the thought processes of key executives," says an insider. Although it may not be wise to highlight this motivation during your interview, a consulting firm is an excellent training ground, regardless of the type of work you ultimately wish to pursue, and many firms work hard to stay in touch with their alumni networks. Consulting gives people a chance to not only learn about different organizations and industries, but also a long list of contacts with whom they can network when they decide they're ready to move on.

WATCH OUT!

A Dog's Life

The travel, the hours, and the difficulty of maintaining a personal life top everyone's list of consulting complaints. "There is limited life outside of work," one insider says. It's not that people in other professions don't work long, hard hours, but the consulting lifestyle, which often requires the consultant to be out of town four days a week for months at a time, is hard to maintain over the long run, especially for people with families. Some individuals actually thrive on the pace and excitement of the frenetic schedule. For many others, a few years are about all they want to put up with.

"I'd rather be…"

Consultants often express their desire to get into the thick of managing a company and start making management decisions. This may be a bit of the "grass is greener" syndrome, but after giving advice to so many companies and executives, many consultants are eager to try their hand from the client side. They also complain about not getting the in-depth experience they'd get if they worked at a company. A large number of consultants leave after a few years to start businesses or work in operating companies.

What difference does it make?

Most people who go into consulting as a career say they do valuable, highly meaningful work. However, a common complaint among ex-consultants is that the work didn't seem as meaningful to them as they would have liked. As one says, "I felt like we did a lot of ephemeral strategy stuff for big companies that didn't really amount to much. I really didn't want to be working with conservative, old Fortune 500 companies. I wanted to be making a difference in a smaller setting, with real people."

Control

No matter how good your advice, there's no guarantee that a client will take it. If you like to see your ideas in action—or like to act on your ideas yourself—you may find a consulting gig frustrating. "At the end of the day, when all's said and done, you're telling somebody else what to do, and you don't have control over it," a consultant says. "You can sometimes feel like your hands are tied when you can't make that decision."

The Long Haul

By one insider's estimate, only one in ten people who start with a consulting firm is really a consultant at heart. As almost anyone who graduated from business school three years ago will tell you, very few classmates remain consultants for long. People leave for a variety of reasons, but most do leave. Therefore, if you're thinking that you'd like to set down roots and have something substantive to show for your work, you'll be better off in another type of organization.

Getting Hired

The Recruiting Process

The Interviewer's Checklist

Interviewing Tips

Grilling Your Interviewer

The Case Interview

Interview Prep

The Aspiring Consultant

What Insiders (and Outsiders) Say

The Recruiting Process

There are two main routes into consulting. One goes directly from campus (undergrad and MBA, primarily) into entry-level positions (analyst or consultant). The other leads from industry into midlevel positions in specific practice groups (aerospace, energy, and financial services), functions (marketing or supply chain management), or technologies.

Most consulting firms follow a fairly standard recruiting routine for undergrads and graduate students. The typical tryout starts with an on-campus interview or two and finishes up with a half day or full day at the office where you want to work. Interviews can be one-on-one or two-on-one and usually include a basic resume review and a lot of questions designed to determine your fit with the organization. In addition, most interviews include every consulting recruiter's favorite fear-inspiring tool: the case interview. In a traditional case interview, the candidate is presented with a business or intellectual problem and asked to reason through the problem to a logical conclusion. These can be fairly complex and typically require the candidate to build on a set of assertions. We'll cover the case interview in more detail later in this chapter.

Competition for consulting spots is intense—major firms review hundreds of resumes for each hire they make. To stand out from the crowd, an impressive school and grades and a demonstration of significant work or leadership experience are usually essential. In almost all cases, prepare to be screened for "fit" with the firm, an elusive personality-based assessment. And remember that consulting is a conservative industry. A pale blue resume, white loafers, and off-color comments will certainly earn you a rejection letter.

Firms will be hiring in 2006–07, and, as always, recruiting will be competitive. If you're serious about a consulting career, know the firms before you talk to them, develop relationships with as many people at each firm as possible, and make sure you get the details right—from proofreading each correspondence to dressing appropriately for your interviews. And have your story down: Know why you want to be a consultant as well as why you want to be a consultant at [insert name of firm here].

"Really understand the work: What is consulting work? What are the skills required to succeed in it? It's general business knowledge, but also interpersonal skills. Spend time getting to know alumni, classmates, and recruiters, so that you can fit in," says a career center director at a top business school. "Secondary to that, for each specific company, really understand what makes it unique. Who are the type of people they hire, and articulate why you would fit in."

"You need to think about whether this is the right job for you," an insider says. "You need to look at the people you meet as you're going through, and decide whether the firms you're interviewing with are places [where] you'd be happy. That usually comes down to the people. If you're not looking at one of the larger, established brand names, you've got to be clear about

> **"Find out which companies typically hire people like you. If you're a business person with a stunning GPA, it's not guaranteed that you'll get interviews."**

their position, where their flow of consulting projects is going to come from. With the established firms, it's probably worth understanding how they've dealt with the last couple of years, how busy people have been, and if the consultants been given sufficient experience."

"You can't go half-hearted," another insider says. "For people who are nontraditional types of hires, especially for humanities majors, find out which companies typically hire people like you. If you're a business person with a stunning GPA, it's not guaranteed that you'll get interviews."

The Interviewer's Checklist

Each interviewer has a different style of presenting a case question. Some try to over-whelm you with detail, while others provide very little and wait to see what the candidate will ask about. In the end, however, most interviewers are trying to assess a few simple things:

- How strong are the candidate's analytical abilities? (Does he think logically? Can she break a problem into component pieces and solve them?)

- How well does the candidate communicate his or her ideas? (Can the person express ideas in a clear and convincing way? Is the candidate able to clearly explain complex ideas?)

- Does the person have presence and poise? (Does the candidate get flustered by questions? Does the candidate seem at ease during the case?)

Although the case interview inspires the most fear among would-be consultants, answers to the above questions are not all that interviewers are looking for. Most pay close attention to a candidate's experience and background. According to insiders, in addition to the qualities they look for in the case interview, most consulting interviewers are looking for the following:

- High energy and enthusiasm

- Team orientation

- Integrity

- Excitement about consulting

- Knowledge about what makes the interviewing firm different

- Success on the airplane test—do you want to sit next to this person on a long overseas flight?

- Interpersonal skills

- Industry experience

- Ethical behavior

- Critical thinking

Interviewing Tips

Although the top management consulting firms hire hundreds of people every year, thousands and thousands of people compete for those positions. There's no surefire way to guarantee an offer, and there are few, if any, back doors into the organizations. In most cases, your best bet will be to go through the standard on-campus recruiting program and bid lots of points to get on those schedules. (Check with your career center on how to "bid points" for interviews.) Beyond that, however, insiders tell us that there are a number of ways you can improve your chances in the interview process. Here are a few of their suggestions about how to prepare for your interviews:

1. Be ready to offer specific examples of how your background and experience have provided you with excellent preparation for a career in consulting. Though most candidates focus on the case question, many blow their chances before they even hear one.

2. Be ready to give a good answer to the question, "Why do you want to go into consulting?" Of course, there is no single right answer to this question, but there are wrong answers. The worst is to say something you don't really believe. Even if you do happen to slip it by the interviewer, you'll pay the price later.

3. Keep a high energy level. Recruiters get tired of asking the same questions, so it's up to you to inject some excitement into the interview. At the end of a long day in the cubicle, chances are good they'll remember more about your enthusiasm than about the bullet points on your resume.

4. Prepare for the case interview. There's no way around it. To get an offer from a consulting firm, you'll need to nail not only one, but as many as eight or ten different case questions during your three rounds of interviews. To do your best, insiders recommend that you attend any informational sessions about the case interview, do some case interview drills with a friend, sign up for mock interviews (if possible), and, of course, refer to the Ace Your Case® series, WetFeet's best-selling management consulting case interview prep guides, available at www.wetfeet.com.

5. Know what distinguishes the firm you're interviewing with from its competitors, and be able to explain why you want to work for them. Everybody knows that most people who want to go into consulting will interview with all the firms. However, you still need to demonstrate that you have enough interest in a particular employer to have done your homework.

6. Practice before the interview. Try to set up mock interviews with a wide variety of people—those in the industry, those you met during your summer internship, and those you're not necessarily comfortable with. "Practice interviewing with people who put you out of your comfort zone," says an insider. "That way you learn your limits and know how you're going to react." Ask for direct feedback from alumni and friends, and tell them not to pull punches. If you really want a job in consulting, you want to be as prepared as you possibly can going into the process. Says an insider, "It all makes a difference."

Grilling Your Interviewer

The following are good generic questions that will fit most consulting interviews. However, you'll want to think of additional ones that specifically apply to the company you're interviewing with. We've grouped our questions according to our sense of their relative risk—use "Well Done" questions with extreme caution.

RARE

- Why did you decide to go into consulting?

- Tell me about a project you worked on and your individual role in the process.

- Can you give me an example of a project that didn't go as well as you had hoped, and tell me what you learned from the experience?

- What have you done for fun lately?

- What are the differences between your offices in [city or country name] and [city or country name]?

- What do you like most about consulting?

- What don't you like about consulting?

- What kinds of people do well at your firm?

MEDIUM

- What measures is your firm taking to increase workplace diversity?

- What is the turnover rate at your firm, and how does that compare with the rest of the industry?

- What things do you like or dislike about your firm?

- If you could work for any one of your competitors, which one would it be and why?

- What are your firm's strategies for building its brand? What are the pros and cons of that strategy?

- How much responsibility will I have on a project team?

- If I were a prospective client, why would I hire you over your competitors?

- What's the difference between a good analyst and a mediocre one?

WELL DONE

- In what areas are your competitors better than you, and what are you doing to catch up?

- Tell me a couple of reasons why I wouldn't want to work for you.

- Is there an Ivy League bias at your firm?

- How's morale at your firm? How does it compare to morale at firms where you have friends? How does it compare to morale a few years ago?

- Do consultants really add value to the companies they advise?

- How can someone just out of school really presume to give advice to a client who has been in the industry for his or her entire career?

- What steps do you take to make sure that your recommendations don't just sit on the client's bookshelf?

- How many female and minority partners are there at your firm?

The Case Interview

In essence, the case interview is nothing more than a simplified business problem designed to serve as a platform for the interviewee to show off his or her problem-solving abilities. It's also something like fraternity hazing. Anyone sitting on the other side of the table has been through it and survived, and, as a result, believes it to be a legitimate means of separating the wheat from the chaff. So, like it or not, you've got to be able to crack the case when it's given to you.

THE SET-UP

The case question usually starts off as a brief description of a typical client problem: "I'm a steel manufacturer, and my revenue is going down." This may be a simplified version of a project from the consultant's own background, or it may be something made up to draw on—or differ from—things on your own resume. In any case, the interviewer will typically provide a package of background information about the company, the industry, and the problem. The recruiter will end with, "What would you do now?"

THE PROCESS

As the applicant works through the answer, the recruiter will continue to provide more details about the case and ask a variety of questions to probe the candidate's thought process. During the course of the discussion, the interviewer might ask the applicant to explain the reasoning behind a particular approach. In other cases, the interviewer might play devil's advocate and challenge the candidate's assertions, or role-play as an unruly and uncooperative client.

WHAT IT MEANS

Although a few firms have bucked the trend by placing considerably less emphasis on the case interview ("Let's face it. Eighty percent of the students at the top schools won't have any problem with the analytics of the job," says one MBA assigned to a recruiting role), most continue to view the case interview as the primary means of determining a candidate's aptitude for the work. The key is not to get the "right" answer, since usually there is no one right answer. Rather, the interviewer is hoping to get some insight into how the applicant thinks and solves problems. For better or worse, many recruiters also see the case question as the Rosetta stone to a person's character, intelligence, sense of humor, background, personal habits, and virtually anything else you want to throw in.

HOW TO ANSWER

Case interview success isn't based on shooting from the hip and solving a highly complex problem in the course of five minutes. Rather, it primarily depends on your thought process and presentation. "The biggest problem in case interviews is that people are too formulaic," one insider tells us. "We've all taken game theory. The students know they should be structured and use a framework. But what we're really looking for is somebody to be organic, to take it to the next level. We know the structure they're going to use, but can they go beyond that? Many students are too rigid. They apply Porter's 5 everywhere—even where it doesn't apply. It's expected, so we won't be impressed."

Interview Prep

The best way to prepare for a consulting interview is to go through a few practice sessions with a friend or a mock interviewer. This will give you invaluable experience in spinning out a quick, cogent, and poised response to a case question and make the unavoidable encounter with one in the interview room that much easier.

TIPS FOR SAILING THROUGH THE CASE INTERVIEW

1. Listen carefully to the material presented. Take notes if you want to, and be sure to ask questions if you are unsure about details.

2. Take your time. Nobody is expected to have a brilliant solution to a complex problem on the tip of his or her tongue. If you need a minute or two to collect your thoughts and work through your answer, say so.

3. Offer a general statement—or framework—up front to serve as an outline for your answer. Although the framework can be something as elaborate as a 3C (customer, company, competition) model, it need not be anything more than, for example: "If you're asking about declining profits, then I'd want to check into factors affecting cost and factors affecting revenue. On the cost side…" As you proceed with your answer, draw on the outline of your framework.

4. Try to focus first on what you think are the key issues in the case. Many interviewers will be checking to see if you operate by the 80/20 rule, which means that you should first address the broader issues that will get you 80 percent of the way to a good solution.

5. Orient your answer toward action. Remember, the goal of a consulting gig is to provide the client with actionable recommendations.

6. Don't be afraid to think out loud. The interviewer is looking as much for evidence of a logical thought process as for a brilliant solution to the case problem.

7. Be conscious of resources. A lot of consulting work is figuring out how you're going to collect the information you need to answer a question—without costing the client a fortune. It's probably not a good idea to suggest interviewing dozens of CEOs to see how they have dealt with similar issues, because setting up those interviews would be a nightmare.

8. Present your answer with conviction. A consultant's success depends largely on his or her ability to convince clients to embark on difficult courses of action. How you present yourself plays a big role in this.

9. Have fun with the case! Consulting is really like a steady succession of case interview questions. If you are going to do well in consulting, you need to enjoy the intellectual challenge of analyzing tough problems and coming up with good answers.

A FEW OPEN-ENDED SAMPLES

To give you a little more wood for the fire, we have provided a few case questions—without answers. In preparing for your interviews, you might try working with a friend to come up with good answers for these questions.

1. A medical device manufacturer is developing a host of new technologies, but must decide where to dedicate its limited financial resources. How would you evaluate the market opportunity for different lines of products?

2. A telecom company provides software for email service on local area networks. Should it expand to provide broader Internet services?

3. A pharmaceutical company has a proprietary drug that is about to lose its patent protection. That means generic substitutes for the product will soon become available at a fraction of the original drug's cost. How would you adjust the price of the product in response?

4. A large car company is considering setting up a new subassembly plant for engine production. Where should it locate the plant? What information do you need to know? How would you get it?

5. Why would the buying cycle for paper products be cyclical? Can you think of other industries with similar patterns?

6. How much money would American Airlines save if, on the LaGuardia-Logan shuttle, it split each can of soda it served between two passengers?

7. A restaurant-owning company is renovating its bathrooms. Should it install hand dryers or paper towel dispensers? What's the cost/benefit for each option? Would your recommendation be affected by how long the restaurant stays in business? Would it be affected by what other restaurants are doing?

The Aspiring Consultant

IS CONSULTING REALLY FOR YOU?

No question about it, an offer from a consulting firm is enough to make any red-blooded MBA (or college grad or PhD or whatever) start salivating. But before you start licking your chops, you ought to figure out whether consulting is really right for you. To that end, why not take our test?

 THE CONSULTING APTITUDE TEST

**Can you see yourself saying—or wanting to say—
any of the following things?**

		Yes!	No Way!
1.	"I've got tickets to the concert of the year tonight, but I really don't mind missing it so I can finish off these slides for tomorrow's presentation."	☐	☐
2.	"I just loved those business school case studies!"	☐	☐
3.	"Just yesterday, I sat down with the CEO of a $10-billion-a-year utility company and was telling him that he ought to…"	☐	☐
4.	"Hello? Is this the Phoenix Ritz-Carlton? Put me in room 224 for another week. See you tomorrow!"	☐	☐
5.	"I really don't mind seeing myself in a Dilbert cartoon."	☐	☐
6.	"I can't think of anything worse than having to sell breakfast cereal day in and day out."	☐	☐

THE CONSULTING APTITUDE TEST

	Yes!	No Way!
7. "I don't have to get public credit for my individual contribution to a project."	☐	☐
8. "I want to be able to pay off my student loans in a hurry."	☐	☐
9. "I love working in teams."	☐	☐
10. "I love working with bright, highly educated, ambitious people." (Translation: "I have no patience working with people who aren't just like me.")	☐	☐
11. "I don't need a job in which the product is something I can touch and feel."	☐	☐
12. "I don't take it personally when one of my ideas gets shot down."	☐	☐
13. "I can hardly wait to get acquainted with the new Xerox machine."	☐	☐
14. "God, I love it when we can save a corporation $20 million with a little bit of creative thinking!"	☐	☐
15. "I thrive in situations where there's a lot of ambiguity."	☐	☐

Scoring the survey. That's right, you guessed it: The more of these quotes you could imagine leaving your lips, the more you want to be a consultant. If very few of these things sit well with you, you really ought to think about going into sales, teaching, politics, or something else. And remember, there's no shame in that. What a boring place the world would be if everyone were a consultant.

WHAT KIND OF FIRM DO YOU WANT TO WORK FOR?

Let's face it. Most consulting firms look a lot alike. They also compete intensely with each other for top candidates. As a result, they all offer excellent pay and perks. Beyond that, however, there are reasons why you might prefer one to another. By encouraging you to think about your personal preferences, the following worksheet should help you identify the type of firm in which you'd fit best.

 ### CONSULTING FIRM APPEAL TEST

1. What are the three or four industries in which you are most interested?

_____

_____

2. In which part of the country or world do you want to work?

_____

3. Where will you not work?

_____

_____

4. In which of the following types of environments would you feel most comfortable?

_____

_____

CONSULTING FIRM APPEAL TEST

Large	Small
Lots of structure	Lack of structure
Strong, well-defined culture	Weak, inchoate culture
Work mostly with other consultants	Work mostly with client staff
Formal	Informal
Work on strategic issues	Work on operational issues
Work on multiple projects at once	Work on one project at a time
Work in lots of different industries	Focus on a specific industry
Follow a defined career path	Create your own path
Prefer to facilitate groups	Prefer to analyze and present findings
Prefer to have an office	Don't mind working out of a suitcase

5. Divide 100 points among the following attributes in order of their importance to you:

_____ Reputation   _____ Location

_____ Pay   _____ Training programs

_____ Fit with people   _____ Size of firm

_____ Work focus   _____ Industry and practice focus

_____ Travel requirements   _____ Attention to work/life balance

_____ Attitude   _____ Other: _____

Interpreting the survey. Made your choices, read the report, and still don't know which firm is best for you? Don't fret. Use this survey to ask the firms—and yourself— the right questions during the interviewing process. That will help you get to the bottom line: Is consulting, and this firm in particular, the right place for me?

What Insiders (and Outsiders) Say

People go into consulting for lots of reasons. After extensive research of the industry and interviews with a number of people who have gone into consulting, as well as those who have decided not to, our impression is that consulting is a great career for a few people, a good short-term job for some, and a bad place for many others.

BEST REASONS FOR GOING INTO CONSULTING

- Good way to learn about lots of industries without committing for life

- Lots of bright, hardworking people like those you know from school

- Good pay, benefits, and perks

- Chance to see the world, even if the tour of duty requires months in Pittsburgh

- Can't decide what else to do with your life

- Virtually a no-lose career option

- Ego—telling CEOs what to do makes you feel important

- Belief that consultants make business and the world a better place

- Debt: You can't afford to turn down the excellent offer they made you

- Want to make a transition from one industry to another

- Strong contact network will help you throughout your career

BEST REASONS FOR NOT GOING INTO CONSULTING

- Having a real life—weekends and evenings free to spend with your significant other, friends, and family

- Want a career, not just an adventure

- Don't want people to get laid off because of your recommendations

- Prefer being on the line and having profit-and-loss responsibility

- Prefer small companies

- Would rather work with one organization and learn specialized skills

- Annoyed by unstructured work with endless course corrections

- Dislike the consulting culture and self-important people

- Don't believe consultants add much value

- Didn't get any callbacks

So, You Might Not Want to Be a Consultant?

If you're thinking that you really aren't cut out to be a consultant, or if you're exploring other options, you might find the next section helpful. We've tried to compare a career in consulting with a couple of other popular options for students coming out of undergraduate and graduate programs.

INVESTMENT BANKING VS CONSULTING

For students at both the undergraduate and graduate levels, two of the most prominent job opportunities are consulting and investment banking. In many ways, the jobs are similar. Both consultants and investment bankers serve as advisors to industry. As a result, there is a strong focus on client service, with the expectation that you will respond to client demands immediately and effectively (personal needs take a backseat). Likewise, both professions require strong analytical abilities, attention to detail, intelligence, and an interest in business issues and the business world.

On another level, however, investment banking and consulting are quite different, and, as a result, attract different types of people. In broad terms, investment bankers' advice focuses on financial issues; consultants deal with a much wider variety of business issues. Investment bankers help clients raise capital, prepare for IPOs, structure deals with other companies, and underwrite debt and equity offerings. The work requires a high level of comfort with numbers and the finance-related fields of accounting, tax, and law.

By contrast, consultants look at a whole range of business issues, from top-level corporate strategy, to marketing programs, to redesigning a firm's back-office operations, to setting up a new MIS (management information system) structure. Although consultants also need to be comfortable with numbers and frequently come into contact with finance issues, they typically spend a lot more time working with client staff to actually implement recommendations they've made. Consequently, they need to enjoy working with a wider range of people and, depending on the firm and its approach, be willing to do more hand-holding with client staff.

Investment Banking vs Consulting

Investment Banking	Consulting
Live and work in New York City, Tokyo, or London	Live in any of a number of cities and work in Peoria, Boise, Tampa, or wherever the client is located
Work 70- to 80-hour weeks with spike times up to 90 hours, weekends usually free	Work 60-hour weeks, with crunch times exceeding 100 hours; work almost every weekend
Fast-paced, deal-oriented work	Long-term, project-oriented work
Balance 15 deals at once, all in different stages of completion	Work on one or two projects at once, complete them, and then take on others
Lower salary but big bonuses—with even bigger rewards for sticking around for a few years	Get paid more at the start, bonuses not as significant
Compensation based on performance, wide variance among individuals, wide swings from year to year	Compensation more equal among people at same level, steady growth, relatively stable from year to year
Focus on numbers, finance, deals	Focus on general business problems, strategy, operations, marketing
Deal primarily with CFOs, CEOs, lawyers	Deal extensively with CEOs and top management, but lots of contact with middle managers and lower-level employees
More opportunity to shine individually	Stronger teamwork orientation
Final product: a contract or prospectus	Final product: a series of presentations and recommendations, often followed by implementation work

INDUSTRY VS CONSULTING

Although many graduates of top universities and MBA programs choose careers in the more glamorous consulting and investment banking industries, most still find work elsewhere. Given the seductive pull of the glitzy presentations given by the consulting firms and banks, chances are good that even if you're thinking about a career in industry, you may be tempted by the consulting world. To help you understand more about the different tracks, here's a summary of representative differences between the two options:

Industry vs Consulting

Company	Consulting Firm
Work primarily with the same group of people	Project teams, colleagues, and clients change every few months
More direct involvement with a product	Arm's-length involvement with client's products
Make management decisions	Suggest management decisions
Deal with a wide range of people and have a direct impact on their daily lives	Deal mostly with senior and mid-level managers; have a large impact on other people, but from a distance
Challenges revolve around getting things done, motivating people, dealing with personnel issues, making operating decisions	Challenges revolve around tackling and understanding complex problems and teaching clients to deal with them
Satisfaction from making product change	Satisfaction from affecting organization and competitiveness
Learn from a mentor with years of industry or functional experience	Learn from a mentor who is closer in age to you and who has consulting experience
With a good education and ambition, you might really stand out	With the most extraordinary accomplishments, you'll just be equal to everybody else
Your reputation and connections develop over months and years	Have to make quick impressions, then move on
Compensation packages generally lower, but you might get stock options	Compensation and perks more attractive

TECHNOLOGY VS CONSULTING

Technology companies have often enticed graduates to sign on with them, dangling stock options, special perks, and the entrepreneurial challenges of working for a technology company or startup. Many of the same differences noted under "Industry vs Consulting" are relevant here, as are the following:

Technology vs Consulting

	Technology	Consulting
Compensation:	Salary and stock options	Salary and bonus
Perks:	Free sodas, great hardware	The Ritz-Carlton
Travel:	Every day in cyberspace, baby	Weekly—have your frequent flyer card ready
Typical dress:	(Almost) anything goes	Gap ads to Brooks Brothers suits
Company parties:	Usually at the office	Biannually in Aspen, Tahiti, or the Caribbean
Competition:	Plenty and brutal	For the best intellectual property
Outlook:	The future of business	The future of business needs paid advisors
Typical workspace:	Messy	Virtual and at the client office
Biggest pain:	Technology	Clients

For Your Reference

Consulting-Speak

General Consulting Information

WetFeet Resources

Consulting Firm Websites

Consulting-Speak

To help prepare you for both your interviews and a possible career in the field, we've asked our insiders to give us the most up-to-date consulting jargon. Beware: Unauthorized use of these terms has been known to seriously offend every known species of consultant.

2x2. Pronounced "two by two," this is a favorite consulting tool used to analyze a number of items along two dimensions. It's basically a graph with X and Y axes that cross in the middle, creating four different sectors. Don't be surprised if you're asked to produce one of these during your interview.

Benchmark. Here's another standard-issue item from the consulting toolbox. Benchmarks are levels of performance or output against which you can evaluate the performance of something else. A benchmark study is an analysis of the performance of a number of companies along specified dimensions. For example, a software firm might hire a consulting firm to do a benchmark study on how much other firms are spending on customer service.

BHAG. Big Hairy Audacious Goal. This buzzword comes from the book *Built to Last* (see next entry).

Built to Last. A book written by James C. Collins and Jerry I. Porras, in which they destroy the myth that the core product is more important than the vision the company espouses. The term now enjoys widespread usage as describing a company with a strong culture based on a core ideology or identity. More loosely, it refers to those firms that want to be around for many decades or centuries, not just a few years.

Business design. Here's a consultant's definition: "For a company, it's not about growing your top line, it's about growing your bottom line." (The bottom line is profit. The top line is sales.) "Business design is about what you do, how you gear up the troops. It has everything to do with whom you hire and what they do. It's your channel, your product, how you execute your offering."

Cactus job. A dull assignment, especially one that's below the consultant's perceived skill set.

Case interview. In a case interview, your interviewer will give you a set of facts and ask you a question to analyze how you structure a problem, think it through, and ultimately come up with a solution. Case questions can be numerical, as in, "How many dimes are currently in circulation?" or business-related, as in, "Suppose a client asked you to figure out why his business is experiencing an unusual decline in sales and a severe cash flow problem." They could also just be wacky, such as, "If Dannon, Yoplait, and Colombo yogurts came to life, what kind of people would they be?"

Change management. Here's a $5 buzzword that sounds like it's making things clear, when really it's just muddying up an already fuzzy concept. Most firms use this term to refer to a specific type of consulting work dedicated to such things as helping a company restructure its organization and cope with the human problems that accompany such an effort.

Convergence. Consulting services in telecommunications (cable, wireless, wireline, and Internet), computers, and media—or "converging" industries. The thinking is that the Internet, the telephone, the TV, the PDA, and the PC will someday all become one.

Core competencies. Things a company does best.

Customer relationship management (CRM). Communication technology that helps companies manage customer information.

Deliverable. The product or solution you give (deliver) to the client. If you promise an analysis of shipping costs, for instance, that's your deliverable. Deliverables typically come with dates (when you will deliver).

Engagement/project/study/case/job. These are all different ways in which the firms refer to a specific project. Interviewers often note which term you use—just to see whether you've read the company literature. Using the wrong word is not an automatic ding, but you'll impress your interviewer if you get it right.

Enterprise resource planning (ERP). An IT solution to streamline operations by connecting all parts of a business electronically—including HR, billing, and inventory. A popular consulting project during the '90s, ERP spurred double-digit annual growth for many firms.

Framework. Basically, a framework is any kind of structure you can use to look at a problem. It can be as simple as, "The company's problems stem from both internal and external factors." Or it can be something more MBA-ish, like Porter's Five Forces. Consultants love frameworks, and the more you use them (up to a point), the more analytical you'll sound.

Growth. From 1997–98 to around 2000, most firms shifted their focus from reengineering—which often meant downsizing—to growth. Growth involved taking a small private start-up from, say, 25 or 30 employees to more than 500 and going public.

Implementation. These days, nobody admits to doing just pure strategy work. The reason? Too many consulting firms were criticized for leaving behind a big stack of slides that never resulted in any action by the client. As a result, all of the firms now talk about how they work with clients to make sure that their expensive analyses and recommendations are actually implemented.

On the beach. In consulting, this refers to any period of time during which you aren't staffed on a project. Although you won't necessarily see any sunshine here, you also won't have to be any place in particular, so there's a chance you'll be able to leave the office early, do your laundry, pay your bills, and maybe even see your honey.

Operations. Operations refers to all of the day-to-day tasks associated with the running of a company. In a manufacturing company, this includes the buying and processing of raw materials as well as the sale and distribution of the final products. Many consulting firms do a big business providing operations advice. At the simplest level, this just means that they help clients run their businesses better.

Outsourcing. To reduce overhead expenses, lots of companies are turning to outsiders to provide many of the functions and services traditionally done in-house. Popular candidates for outsourcing include accounting services, marketing communications, payroll management, and data processing. Increasingly, public firms are turning to these services because they create stable revenue flows, which their investors like.

Pay-for-performance. Billing based on performance, rather than strictly on hours.

Presentation. In the traditional consulting project, the presentation was the means by which a consulting firm shared all of its insights and recommendations with a client company. The client's top management team would assemble in a boardroom, and a partner or case team manager would spin through dozens of overhead slides displaying all of the analysis his or her firm had completed. Although the standard overhead slideshow is now considered a bit sterile, it's still a popular drill at most firms.

Reengineering. Reengineering lost its cachet in the mid-'90s. In its purest sense, a reengineering project was supposed to involve a complete rethinking of a company's operations from ground zero.

Shareholder value analysis. The goal of many companies is to enhance their value to shareholders, and they engage lots of consulting firms to help them do it. There are all manner of ways, proprietary and not, to analyze shareholder value.

Scribe. To take notes. Welcome to your summer internship and your first year on the job.

Socialize. Use strong-arm tactics to gain consensus: "Socialize the client into accepting the recommendation."

True north. The place you want to get to. If you're heading true north, you're moving in the right direction.

Value chain analysis. An analysis of all of the processes that go into a product, from the gathering of raw materials needed to make the product to the delivery of the final product to the customer. At best, each stage adds value to the product.

Virtual office/hoteling. Sexy terms for an office setup in which nobody has a personal desk or office. Means you could be hanging out with the clerks at Kinko's.

White-space opportunity. A money-making opportunity in an area you aren't set up to make money in. Think of it as an unbridged gap between what you do and what others do, or an untapped source of growth.

General Consulting Information

A general resource for information about the consulting industry is *Consultants News*, published by Kennedy Information. For more information about this and other Kennedy publications, visit ConsultingCentral.com or the Kennedy Information website, www.kennedyinfo.com.

Reading *Fast Company, Fortune, Forbes, BusinessWeek, Business 2.0*, the *Wall Street Journal*, and the *New York Times* is an easy way to stay up-to-date on the latest events and issues that management consultants address, and will arm you with plenty of information for your interviews. Each of these publications has a corresponding website that's worth a visit.

WetFeet Resources

Visit WetFeet to get help on everything from finding the right firm to acing your case. At www.wetfeet.com, you will find

- Articles—and even entire guides—on writing killer cover letters and resumes.

- Tips on putting your best foot forward in your interviews.

- Guides to specific firms.

- An in-depth insider series on how to ace your case interviews.

- Plus a wide range of topical information relevant to your job search.

Consulting Firm Websites

Consulting firms regularly publish white papers, studies, and articles as a way to market and promote their services and expertise, educate their clients, and share best practices. If you're interested in a specific firm, take some time to explore its website for information relevant to the practice area you're going into—look for a tab called something like "ideas," "publications," "executive insight," or "thought leadership." Explore what they've published so that you can speak intelligently about their published work in your interview. Here's a selective list of URLs to some of the better publications sections of strategy firms.

Accenture: http://www.accenture.com/Global/Research_and_Insights/default.htm
Notes: Check out *Outlook*, Accenture's online journal of high-performance business.

A.T. Kearney: www.atkearney.com/main.taf?p=5
Notes: *Executive Agenda* is its flagship publication.

Bain: www.bain.com/bainweb/publications/publications_overview.asp
Notes: Take a look at the "Best of Bain."

BearingPoint: www.bearingpoint.com/library/index.html
Notes: Search for articles by industry or by solution.

Boston Consulting Group: www.bcg.com/publications/publications_splash.jsp
Notes: Cool searchable database lets you find articles by industry, topic, publication type, language, or keyword.

Booz Allen Hamilton: www.strategy-business.com
Notes: Booz Allen's well-regarded quarterly, *strategy+business*.

Deloitte: www.deloitte.com/dtt/section_home/0,2331,sid%253D16695,00.html
Notes: Sign up for email research alerts.

McKinsey & Company: www.mckinsey.com/ideas
Notes: Don't miss the *McKinsey Quarterly*.

Mercer Management Consulting: www.mercermc.com/defaultFlash.
asp?section=Perspectives
Notes: Check out the *Mercer Management Journal*.

Monitor Group: www.gbn.com
Notes: Global Business Network, a Monitor company, features excellent future-oriented perspectives on business.

WETFEET'S INSIDER GUIDE SERIES

Job Search Guides

Be Your Own Boss

Changing Course, Changing Careers

Finding the Right Career Path

Getting Your Ideal Internship

International MBA Student's Guide to the U.S. Job Search

Job Hunting A to Z: Landing the Job You Want

Killer Consulting Resumes!

Killer Cover Letters & Resumes!

Killer Investment Banking Resumes!

Negotiating Your Salary & Perks

Networking Works!

Interview Guides

Ace Your Case®: Consulting Interviews

Ace Your Case® II: 15 More Consulting Cases

Ace Your Case® III: Practice Makes Perfect

Ace Your Case® IV: The Latest & Greatest

Ace Your Case® V: Return to the Case Interview

Ace Your Case® VI: Mastering the Case Interview

Ace Your Interview!

Beat the Street®: Investment Banking Interviews

Beat the Street® II: I-Banking Interview Practice Guide

Career & Industry Guides

Careers in Accounting

Careers in Advertising & Public Relations

Careers in Asset Management & Retail Brokerage

Careers in Biotech & Pharmaceuticals

Careers in Brand Management

Careers in Consumer Products

Careers in Entertainment & Sports

Careers in Health Care

Careers in Human Resources

Careers in Information Technology

Careers in Investment Banking

Careers in Management Consulting

Careers in Marketing & Market Research

Careers in Nonprofits & Government Agencies

Careers in Real Estate

Careers in Retail

Careers in Sales

Careers in Supply Chain Management

Careers in Venture Capital

Industries & Careers for MBAs

Industries & Careers for Undergrads

Million-Dollar Careers

Specialized Consulting Careers: Health Care, Human Resources, and Information Technology

Company Guides

25 Top Consulting Firms

25 Top Financial Services Firms

Accenture

Bain & Company

Booz Allen Hamilton

Boston Consulting Group

Credit Suisse First Boston

Deloitte Consulting

Deutsche Bank

The Goldman Sachs Group

J.P. Morgan Chase & Co.

McKinsey & Company

Merrill Lynch & Co.

Morgan Stanley

UBS AG

WetFeet in the City Guides

Job Hunting in New York City

Job Hunting in San Francisco